PRAISE FOR
WE ANSWERED THE CALL

Every country needs at least one place where its national values live and grow every day in the hearts of people sworn to protect them. With wonderful self-effacing humor, Jim Wilhite tells his tale of uprooting from a normal American life to help with Afghanistan's brave attempt to build such a place. Along with the personal heartache, culture shock, and ridiculous snafus that come with any endeavor as big as this one, Wilhite perfectly captures how the new Military Academy was born out of the pragmatic sense of right and unbeatable spirit that Afghan and American military people share. His story ought to give us all hope that the end of current events in Afghanistan will be good for the whole world.

—Colonel Eugene Ressler
Professor United States Military Academy
Department Head: Department of Computer Science

COL James Wilhite writes a remarkable account of the birth of the National Military Academy of Afghanistan. His leadership and efforts in developing the NMAA during those early days is directly responsible for the absolute success of the Academy today. His vision set the direction for the greatest capacity-building event for the country of Afghanistan. The NMAA is developing the future leaders of character and competence for the Afghan National Army and the country of Afghanistan. It can be truly said that COL James Wilhite is the "father" of the NMAA. Thank goodness he "answered the call."

—Colonel Edward Naessens
Professor United States Military Academy
Department Head: Department of Physics

This is the amazing tale of the founding of the "West Point of Afghanistan". Plucked from his position as a college professor and dropped into the middle of a war torn nation, author Jim Wilhite, a U.S. Army Reserve Colonel and a true American hero, recounts his surprisingly humorous yet gripping adventures in the establishment of the critically important National Military Academy of Afghanistan. You will not be able to put *We Answered the Call* down.

—Colonel David Wallace
Professor United States Military Academy
Deputy Department Head: Department of Law

Incumbent with my job as the Dean of the US Army Command and General Staff College, I read many of the books on the wars in Iraq and Afghanistan, or at least I start them. This book is different. Foremost, it is a book that you will not be able to put down because the people from this story will grab hold and pull you in. It is an absolutely true story totally immersed in the human dimension of war. It offers a glimpse of a brave but destitute Afghan people. Most uniquely, this story tells a story of soldiering as it has not often discussed, the story of the humanity of the American soldier as imbued in 'Team Has Been.' Here is a bunch of old guys that should have been back home enjoying their discount at Denny's. Now, half way around the world in a city of 3 million people, several of whom don't like them a lot, we have the perfect conditions for a group of guys with really bad attitudes. What you will find is an uplifting saga that will make you feel good about the American spirit as it should be. Jim Wilhite tells this tale magnificently with the same passion and humor that is the spirit of the man. Thanks to Jim for sharing this experience with others. And personally, I want to thank you for leaving out a couple of the grosser moments of which I may have had some culpability. Carry on.

—Dr. W. Chris King
Brigadier General, US Army (retired)
Dean of Academics
US Army Command and General Staff College
Ft. Leavenworth, KS

Tom,

Thank you for your service & friendship over the years.

God Bless You
&
God Bless America!

2/27/2013

COL. JAMES WILHITE, USA (RET.)

WE ANSWERED THE CALL

BUILDING THE CROWN JEWEL OF AFGHANISTAN

TATE PUBLISHING & Enterprises

Published by Tate Publishing & Enterprises, LLC
127 E. Trade Center Terrace | Mustang, Oklahoma 73064 USA
1.888.361.9473 | www.tatepublishing.com

Tate Publishing is committed to excellence in the publishing industry. The company reflects the philosophy established by the founders, based on Psalm 68:11,
"The Lord gave the word and great was the company of those who published it."

Book design copyright © 2010 by Tate Publishing, LLC. All rights reserved.
Cover design by Amber Gulilat
Interior design by Stephanie Woloszyn

More than 13,000 photos were taken to document the extent of this mission. Photos included in this book were contributed by: MSG Joe Johnson and MAJ Fred Rice, OMC-A PAO, Colonels Chris King, Buck Buchanan, Ray Nelson, Barry Shoop, David Wallace, Ray Winkel, Lieutenant Colonel Doug Hays, and Dr. Larry Butler. Thank you for helping document one of the many outstanding missions in Afghanistan.

Published in the United States of America

ISBN: 978-1-61566-779-6
1. History / Military / Afghan War (2001-) 2. Biography & Autobiography / Military
11.03.21

THIS BOOK IS DEDICATED TO MY WIFE, EMILY,
AND OUR GIRLS, SARAH AND LAURA.
THANK YOU FOR SUPPORTING ME, OUR TROOPS,
AND THIS EXTREMELY IMPORTANT MISSION.
I LOVE YOU GIRLS!

P.B./DAD/PADRE

ACKNOWLEDGMENT

Of all the work I have done on this book, I consider the acknowledgments portion to be the most difficult. There were so many people that encouraged me with their words, feelings and actions that to have not completed this book would have been a disappointment to them. I want to mention just a few of the individuals and share their interest in my work.

Vincent Viola, a West Point Graduate, attended the grand opening of the academy with Brigadier General Kaufman's staff. Vincent stayed with me for three days and strongly encouraged me to pursue the book option. He also did an initial reading on one of my early drafts and provided valuable feedback.

Lieutenant Colonel (Ret) Craig Roberts, a noted author, also provided significant feedback on a later piece of work and told me to broaden my efforts to a larger audience. He felt this story needed to be told to more than just military personnel.

Dr. Tom Newton and his son Brooks: Both read my final work as non-military individuals and provided information that greatly enhanced my writing style as well as providing the non-military view of what was being written.

To the faculty and staff at West Point, as well as in the other services that assisted me with this mission. There are too many to mention in the acknowledgment portion of this book, but their names and actions are explained in great detail throughout the mission.

To the strangers that heard my stories, either at presentations or in more informal surroundings. The common thread was, "You need to write a book and share your experiences with people." Thank you for that encouragement.

To my family members at the reunions that continued the encouraging words.

Last but not least to my wife and children. Thank you for your continued support and putting up with my nonsense as I, at times, struggled with the story that I wanted to tell.

TABLE OF CONTENTS

FOREWORD

I was sitting in my study at home on a beautiful fall Saturday morning in 2003 reading email before taking on the day's "honey-do" chores. One email caught my attention, "Let's talk on Monday," wrote my boss, Brigadier General Dan Kaufman, Dean of the Academic Board at West Point. The attached email chain contained a request for assistance from then Major General Karl Eikenberry, Chief of the Office of Military Cooperation-Afghanistan, to Lieutenant General William J. Lennox, Jr., West Point Superintendent. General Eikenberry, who was responsible for building the new Afghan National Army, was asking for West Point's assistance in establishing a military academy to educate officers for this new army in this emerging democracy. I immediately hit reply and typed the following response, "Send me; I'm qualified for this mission." I was, at the time, a Permanent Professor at the United States Military Academy and Vice Dean for Education. Aside from assignments in Germany and Korea, I had devoted my entire career to officer education at the Military Academy. I was eager to make a contribution to the current operations, and this was the perfect opportunity. Turning off the computer, I calmly told my wife that I had just volunteered to go to a combat zone to create a school.

On October first, Lieutenant Colonel Casey Neff, a West Point colleague, and I landed in Kabul, Afghanistan. General Eikenberry had departed days before, so we reported to his replacement, Brigadier General Joe Prasek, who gave us our mission: develop a concept plan for a new National Military Academy of Afghanistan to be up and running in fifteen months. I was to lead an international team that included a Turkish officer, four translators, and ten Afghan officers. We were to be part of a multinational and joint team that was designing the Afghan National Army and Ministry of Defense. We were given six weeks and a blank sheet of paper to come up with the plan.

On November 11, 2003, our team presented the plan to the Afghan Minister of Defense and senior civilian and military leaders. Our team's report offered a comprehensive operational and organizational concept plan for the National Military Academy of Afghanistan. To implement the plan, we recommended that the U.S. Army identify a senior reserve officer with a background in education who could deploy to Afghanistan for a year to make the concept a reality. Colonel Jim Wilhite, Professor of Education at Northeastern State University in Oklahoma, got the call, and the Army could not have made a better choice.

Conception is relatively quick and exciting; birth and delivery are considerably more work. This is the story of the birth and delivery of the National Military Academy of Afghanistan (NMAA). Jim would be the first to say that NMAA had many parents and hundreds of aunts and uncles, and he would be correct. West Point's leadership embraced this mission, and staff and faculty from West Point, and later from the U.S. Air Force Academy, have deployed to Kabul to be part of this important effort. In fact, an academy staff and faculty member has been in Kabul since Casey Neff and I arrived in 2003.

Everyone on the American team would also be quick to point out that NMAA would not be possible without the dedication and courage of our Afghan colleagues, both military and civilian. Those of us who supported this effort never forgot that Afghanistan is their country and NMAA is their academy. We were privileged to walk alongside our Afghan friends as we collaborated on this complex project. Most of us would confess that we learned more from our Afghan partners than they learned from us, and we were simply honored to be part of this grand experiment.

True enough, the National Military Academy of Afghanistan had a large international family, but Jim Wilhite delivered the baby into the world. He provided the drive and indefatigable determination to bring the academy to life. His educational acumen, iron will, and country-boy sense of humor and charm were the perfect mix for this challenging mission. He brought Afghans, Turks, and Americans together. He fought for the resources and adapted the plan to the immediate realities. He worked the angles, drank the chai, and made the friends that were necessary to bring the concept to life. The reader will find all this and more in his compelling account of what may well be the crown jewel of Operation Enduring Freedom. NMAA opened its doors in February 2005, fifteen months after the plan was accepted, and its first class graduated four years later in January 2009. This is a remarkable achievement, and the credit belongs to many dedicated people. But it is Jim's story to tell, and he tells it with all the gusto he invested in NMAA. Tashakor, Jim. Thank you.

—George B. Forsythe, Ph.D.
Brigadier General, USA (retired)
President, Westminster College
Fulton, Missouri
June, 2009

INTRODUCTION

As a professor of Education at a small university in Oklahoma, I prepared future teachers in elementary education and loved my job. My wife, Emily, and I were a few years away from retirement, had our home paid for, our children were grown and doing well with their lives. We had very few bills, and good health for the entire family. Everything was perfect, almost!

Spring break was over and I was to have my students conduct presentations for their class projects. I was also beginning preparations with them for their final examinations, which would be administered the first week of May.

On the afternoon of March 24, 2004, I went home to grab a quick sandwich and to check the mail. In my mailbox was a manila envelope from the Human Resources Command in St. Louis. It was no big deal; as an Army reservist I had received those envelopes many times before. However, this particular one was a bit different.

This is a very honest summary of what I experienced, both good and bad. However, if you are looking for a book that slams the efforts of our country, this book is not for you. While there were issues, this book tells the positive side of an experience in a war zone. This may be the only place where you read about such an event. I hope you enjoy reading good news with humor intertwined throughout.

The contents in the envelope were to change my life for the next year. Little did I know that I was about to embark on the most important military mission of his my thirty-seven plus years in the Army Reserve.

YOU HAVE GOT
TO BE KIDDING ME!

What a beautiful day we were having. It was hard to imagine a more picturesque day in Oklahoma. It was the kind of day that makes me sit back and reflect on just how lucky I am to live in such a great country. We had blue skies, a light, warm breeze, and the grass was starting to turn green, which officially kicked off the spring season. Shortly, the Azalea Festival in the neighboring town of Muskogee, Oklahoma, would be in full bloom, which would further magnify this Northeastern Oklahoma landscape. What a day!

I had just completed teaching my courses at the university and stopped by the house for a quick bite to eat and to check our mail. That was the basic routine I would do during the week. If I wasn't having a power lunch with my colleague, Dr. Louis White, I would make the quick stop by the house. I loved watching the History Channel while eating a sandwich and relaxing before heading back to the office. Little did I know that my life was about to take an abrupt change. I was about to go from college professor to active army Colonel doing God knows what!

I had been a member of the Army Reserves for the past thirty-seven plus years and had very much enjoyed my experiences. I attribute much of my success in my civilian world to those experiences in the military. I had spent twelve years as a noncommissioned officer (NCO) before I was commissioned in October of 1979. I had held the rank of Sergeant First Class and had been a drill sergeant for ten years.

On two different occasions, I had been selected as the Division Drill Sergeant of the year and had competed in the national finals in Ft. Monroe, Virginia, where I had placed first runner-up in the competition. I loved my time as a drill sergeant; because the primary focus in that role was that of a teacher, my profession in civilian life. I could see instant success and also instant failure in my troops. At no other time in my military career did I have such a close teaching opportunity as I did as a drill sergeant. I have spoken at many basic training graduations and have made the following observation: "You will meet many people while in the military during your career. Many of those people you will establish a basic relationship with, but may, for some reason, forget their names. However, you will never forget the name of your drill sergeant!"

When I make a comment like that to anyone who is in the military, they usually immediately tell me who their drill sergeant was. That individual will make a lasting impression on a solider as they usher the individual into the military style of living. It always amazed me as to what grown men would do to try to get the praise of the drill sergeant. It reminded me of a little kid trying to get approval. By the way, my drill sergeants were SSG Hayward Wallace and SFC Howard Rankin. It is because of them that I wanted to eventually become a drill sergeant.

In 1978, I had reached a crossroads in my military career and had to make a decision as to what my future would hold for me if I continue on this path. I had been given great guidance by some outstanding noncommissioned officers as well as some officers who helped me make a valued decision. Probably the one non-commissioned officer that encouraged me to consider the officer corps was my first sergeant, Donald Baker. For some reason, he took me under his wing and encouraged me to do anything and everything I could to become a better NCO as well as a better officer. With his guidance, I was commissioned as a first lieutenant in the Army Reserves in October, 1979. Normally, I would have been commissioned a second lieutenant, but I was too old for that rank and had a very good career in the military. I had received my doctorate from Oklahoma State University in school administration and had demonstrated numerous leadership opportunities as a noncommissioned officer (NCO). Based on that record, I was accepted as a first lieutenant.

As I progressed through the ranks to Colonel, I held such positions as Training Officer, Company Commander, Liaison Officer for the Federal Republic of Germany, Instructor for both the Officer Advance Course and the Command General Staff College, Inspector General, and Battalion Commander, finishing my career as a Military Admissions Liaison Officer (MALO) for the United States Military Academy at West Point. I basically had a successful career as an army reservist while at the same time working my way through administrative positions in the public school systems of Oklahoma, until I was selected as an assistant professor at Northeastern State University, in Tahlequah, Oklahoma in 1982.

It was while on the faculty at NSU that I obtained the rank of Colonel in the Army Reserves and began working as a Military Admissions Liaison Officer (MALO) for the academy at West Point. I had the privilege of meeting the best and brightest high school students in Oklahoma who were interested in making the military a career and wanted to attend West Point. It was a dream job to say the least. I was definitely in a win/win situation.

I knew that ninety plus percent of the students I visited with would not be accepted to West Point. While the students had the intelligence, they faced a daunting admissions process which would see over 20,000 applications for 1,400 invitations. Only five percent of the original applications would be invited to become members of "The Long Gray Line."

However, many students that have an interest in the military can obtain their degree through other means besides the service academies. As I talked to students about West Point, I also shared with them the possibilities of university reserve officer training courses (ROTC) and was able to recruit students to assist our NSU/ROTC program, which became quite successful in its own right. We were able to pursue the best and brightest students for our program at Northeastern State University.

MY WORLD CHANGED!

On that fateful day in March, 2004, when I checked the mail, I noticed inside the clear cover of the big manila envelope the following partial statement:

"Pursuant to Presidential Executive Order of 14 Sep 2001, you are relieved from your present reserve component status and ..."

That was all I could read. Immediately, I thought, "Who did I upset? Did I do something inappropriate?" I literally did not understand what I was reading. Of course, I was reading through the small opening in the front of the envelope and could not view the entire message.

As soon as I got in the house I opened the envelope and continued to read.

"... reserve component status and ordered to report for a period of active duty not to exceed 25 days for mobilization processing."

At point I stopped reading and thought to myself, *"Oh, they are calling me to do an annual training (two to three weeks) with some mobilization unit."* I put the letter down and looked through the other mail. I was about to leave and return to the university when I decided to read the rest of the mail mobilization order. After all, the twenty-five days could be a potential problem, since my wife, Emily, and I were planning on going to Hawaii during the upcoming summer. *No problem,* I thought, *we could schedule around those "two to three weeks."*

I read on...

> *"Proceed from your present location in sufficient time to report by the date specified. If upon reporting for active duty you fail to meet deployment medical standards then you may be released from active duty, returned to your prior reserve status and returned to your home address, subject to a subsequent order to active duty upon resolution of the disqualifying medical condition."*

As I had just successfully completed my military physical a few months ago and was hitting on all cylinders, I knew that would not be a factor. I read on...

> *"If, upon reporting for active duty, you are found to satisfy medical deployment standards, then you are further ordered to active duty for a period not to exceed (see period of active duty below) days, such a period to include the period (not to exceed 25 days) required for mobilization processing."*

I was doing fine until I got to the last couple of statements. The part about "further ordered to active duty" and "see period of active duty below." I was gaining interest as to when and where I was to report for this short duration. Two or three weeks as a Colonel represent a nice additional paycheck for a school teacher. So I read down the document/orders.

"Report to: Ft. Benning, Ga."—I knew that place; I am infantry and have spent some time there during my career.

"Report date: No later than 24 Apr 2004 but no earlier than 22 Apr 2004"—Rats, that is just at the end of the semester for my students and just prior to their final exams. I will have to get someone

23

to sub for my classes and give the finals. I should be home in a couple of weeks and can turn in the grades at that time.

Period of Active Duty: Not to exceed 545 days unless extended or terminated by proper authority. "What? You have got to be kidding me!"

Five hundred and forty-five days equals eighteen months, not two to three weeks. I cannot begin to explain what was going through my mind. I may have been hitting on all cylinders from my physical, but after reading the orders I think I burned a cylinder or two. I couldn't get out of my chair. Yes, I was in the IRR. I knew that active duty was a possibility, and if ordered, I would go; however, there was one major issue that I had never even considered if this happened: How do you break the news to your bride of thirty-one years?

Emily was at school and I certainly did not want to go there and break the news in front of all those witnesses. However, as I reflect on the situation now, it might have been safer for me. There was no way I would call her and break the news over the phone. It could, however, give me about a five minute head start before she came home to alter my medical condition and adjust or eliminate what cylinders I had left.

I decided the best option was to not be at the house when she got home. After three or four months, she might start missing me and would be relieved to find out I was still alive some place yet to be determined. However, common sense told me that was really not an option.

I contacted the Dean and the Associate Dean of the College of Education and the Department Head for Curriculum and Instruction to break the news to them first. I had to tell someone. This type of news you can't keep to yourself. We had a lot of class scheduling and changes to be made, and a very short period of time to do it. Enrollment for the next semester had already begun, and many of our classes were full. Also, I had to make arrangements for my students who were currently in my courses. Finals were going to be a potential problem.

I read the orders to Dr. Kay Grant, Dean of the College of Education and Dr. Roxanne Fillmore, Department Head for Curriculum and Instruction. The reaction I got was not surprising. They looked at me like I was going to another planet. They were closer to correct than I could realize. Fortunately, they understood the seriousness of the document and immediately went to work making schedule and personnel adjustments. At this point, I have to say that I work for one of the best institutions in the country. Northeastern State University could not have been more supportive from the President on down, and I will forever be grateful for that support.

I worked out solutions with the Dr.'s Grant and Fillmore and felt comfortable with their plan of action. Now my next issue was to tell Emily about how our lives were about to change. As I was walking out the door of the education building my cell phone rang.

"Hi honey, how was your day?" It was Emily!

"Sweetheart, you have got to come home. I need to talk to you."

"Is everything okay? Are the girls okay?"

"Everyone is fine, I just need to talk to you."

"Well, I am busy at school, can you stop by?"

"No."

"Why not?" Silence followed at this point. "Okay, I will be home in a little bit."

One hour passed and Emily had still not arrived. That was an extremely long hour. I felt like I was in the movie, "The Day the Earth Stood Still." The phone rang and Emily informed me that she was extremely busy and would appreciate it if I just told her over the phone what the problem was.

"I just received orders today calling me to active duty for Operation Enduring Freedom for 545 days and I am to report to Ft. Benning no later than the twenty-fourth of April."

Emily worked at a school about five minutes from our house. I heard the click of the phone hanging up and almost immediately heard the garage door start to open. I went to the garage and she was getting out of the car. According to our initial conversation just a few seconds ago, she was still at school when she called. I will go to my grave trying to figure out how she got home so quickly.

"What do you mean you got called to active duty? You volunteered for this didn't you?" Emily was extremely upset and rightfully so. We had been married for thirty-one years and nothing like this had ever happened before. As much as I tried to convince her that I didn't "volunteer," the deeper the hole I dug for myself.

I had mentioned to her a couple of years ago about being on the "Big Board" for call up, and the possibility of being called up was higher now that I was in the IRR (Individual Ready Reserve) than when I was with a TPU (Troop Program Unit). However, I would not volunteer, and besides, I thought I was too old and had too much rank to be called to active duty.

It was a very long thirty days before I reported. We went through all kinds of emotions and said things that we both would later regret, because we didn't realize just how much we were hurting each other.

For example, during one of our heated conversations I became angry enough to make the following statement, "You have been on my back so much since this happened that I am beginning to look forward to leaving!"

That was about as terrible a comment as I could have said. My life has always involved humor and a little humor here might have helped ease the tension. There was not another person that supported my military career better than Emily and I had driven a stake right into her heart. How could I have been so cruel?

We both stared in silence at each other. I think we were both shocked as to my words. After what seemed to be an eternity I broke into tears and grabbed Emily and apologized. I had thought it, but never thought I would say it. I just didn't realize how those words would hurt the woman I loved, and who was the best thing that ever happened in my life. For that I am truly sorry. Fortunately for me, Emily is a very forgiving person and with her forgiveness and patience we were able to work through our words and feelings. She put on a brave front for our friends and colleagues but I know she was a nervous wreck on the inside. Her way of coping with the situation was to remain calm and poised while I used humor to get me through the day to day questions that had started to bombard us both.

We went through the rest of the month saying our good-byes to everyone that we knew and answering the same question over and over. "Where are you going?" All I knew was that I had to report to Ft. Benning, Georgia, and from there was anybody's guess. However, I was confident that Ft. Benning would be able to inform me immediately as to where my assignment was and when I would be departing. After all, I am a Colonel, and they would have never called me up if they didn't have a special mission designed for me. So I left Tahlequah with a message to my family that I would be calling them in a few days to let them know where I would be. I deserve that respect to at least be informed.

Boy was I wrong!

WELCOME TO CRC

Continental United States Redeployment Center (CRC) at Fort Benning, Georgia, is one of the in-processing sites for soldiers deploying overseas, primarily to Operation Enduring Freedom (Afghanistan), but also for some soldiers to Operation Iraqi Freedom (Iraq). CRC also redeployed people back from overseas to other assignments or to their homes. The Center also deployed civilians and language specialists for necessary operations.

I consider CRC one of the worst jobs in the Army. While it is an extremely important job, I rarely heard a positive statement come from anyone who went through that center. Comments like, "I don't mind doing another year in Iraq/Afghanistan, but I just don't want to have to go through CRC again," were not unusual. The bottom line was that the personnel at CRC were doing their assigned jobs, but they were not taking into consideration the soldiers they were processing.

Many of the soldiers were active duty or guard/reserve personnel. Prior to arriving at CRC, they had been processed through their home station for their paperwork and necessary documents that would make this deployment process a bit smoother. Also, they knew in advance where they were going. Some had been notified two or three months earlier as to their final destination. Their jobs and responsibilities were still in a flex state, but at least they knew they were either going to Afghanistan or Iraq.

However, St. Louis started the Individual Ready Reserve (IRR) call up and that involved people who were in civilian life one month and the next month were deploying to a combat zone. The only information they had received were their orders and a basic packet or document. I thought I was the only one in this situation, but found out through my own investigation that there were others also at CRC with similar questions and concerns.

When I arrived at CRC, I was handed a black folder that had a significant number of stations to visit. Most of these stations were in one big building that was filled with soldiers scrambling around trying to get their paperwork completed. As I was beginning my in-processing, I noticed I was about the only one that had a black folder, perhaps because I was a Colonel and had special privileges or for some other reason. I later discovered it was for some other reason.

I knew I was in trouble when I went to the first station and handed my paperwork to the nice lady. "Who'd you upset?" was her comment. I said that I didn't know, but if she could get me names, I would take them out first! "Most of the people coming through here are only on orders for one year, and yours indicates eighteen months. Where are you going?"

"I don't know. I contacted the Human Resources Command (HRC) in St. Louis to ask them just that, and they said they did not know."

That was a message I heard for seven weeks. The four weeks I had my initial orders, then three weeks plus at CRC I got the "I don't know" answer from everyone I talked to. They couldn't/

wouldn't tell me. In fact, I got the "Where are you going?" question a lot while at CRC. They didn't know where I was going and neither did I.

My mind was racing with scenarios that would have made all my friends and family proud. Was this a secret mission? Was I going to be a diplomat for some foreign mission? Was I going to lead a brigade of soldiers into battle? Was I going to be in charge of Latrine (bathroom) duty for some high ranking general? The truth is, the Army had called me to active duty, disrupted my life, put my marriage in jeopardy, separated me from my family for a possible eighteen months unless I was "extended or relieved by proper authority," brought me to this facility to in-process me to a country or war zone and no one could tell me where I was going! They kept asking me, like it was my idea.

Seventeen others in the room of three hundred plus also had black folders, and eventually we all came together, without the help or guidance of anyone at CRC. Eye contact would be made and we would hold up our folders and gravitate toward each other. Maybe it was the confused look on our faces that drew us together, like a moth to a flame. Also, because we knew absolutely no one at the site, the commonality of the black folder was a way of introduction. We were all grasping at straws to understand the situation.

Through my conversations with the other "Black Folder" soldiers, we discovered a commonality of what made us different from those with regular manila folders. If you had a black folder, then you were from the Individual Ready Reserve and had been called from civilian life and back to active duty for eighteen months, not twelve months like the others in the room. We were a special group. We knew that, because eventually we were told that we were special. As one of our "black folder" members, Colonel Pete Petroski, stated a couple of days later, "Yea, we're special alright. We rode the short bus to school and wore hockey helmets even though we don't have a hockey team!"

We became our own "Band of Brothers" through the black folders. As mentioned earlier, there were eighteen of us, with five being full Colonels and down the ranks to Specialists. We found out very quickly if we were to mentally survive this circus we were about to endure, it would be absolutely necessary for us to stick together.

We gathered together at one of the gazebos in the area and soon discovered that we might have all been married to the same woman. If nothing else, they all had the same conversation with their wives that I had with mine. To the person, everyone that was married had trouble explaining to their spouse they had not volunteered for this mission. They had to defend the emotions they were exhibiting. To a man they tried to put a strong front up for their spouse and suffered the consequences for their lack of communication. They were accused by their spouse of looking forward to this deployment to parts unknown. They all said something that they immediately regretted. Most were able to overcome such comments but a few left with bitterness and emotions that might have been unable to mend.

As we sat around telling about how we got there and some of our experiences with our spouses, the comment, "Are you married to my wife?" came out frequently. It was actually good to know that I was not the only one that had been going through the separation pains with my wife. It was also a good feeling to know that as I left, my relationship with Emily was very strong. However, I was concerned about a couple of my new friends and their chances of making it through this deployment with their marriage unscathed. My concerns bore fruit during the deployment as some of my battle buddies started to return home on leave.

None of us had a clue as to where we were going. In the military, that type of information is prime fuel for the rumor mill to run wild, and it certainly did in this situation. We did not know if we would be deployed together or separately. Regardless of the outcome, we decided that our small team would stick together while at CRC and make sure each individual would be taken care of and not fall through the cracks of the system.

There was one individual who was not one of the "black folders" who seemed to latch on to us. He had a very good idea as to where he was going and bragged continually to us as to his status. He drove us nuts. He was proud of the fact that he knew someone in the Pentagon that would help him with his deployment. He had gotten his branch changed from infantry to quartermaster and was going to be stateside. After a few weeks, we pinned him down and drug his source out of him. He said his wife. She would take care of him and make sure he got a stateside assignment. She took care of him alright; a couple of days later, he shipped out to Iraq. I guess his marriage was not as strong as he thought it was. I wish I could say that I felt guilty about his being sent to Iraq, but I didn't. In fact, we got quite a chuckle after he deployed. We had to look for humor anywhere we could.

WE HAVE OFFICIALLY JOINED A CIRCUS

Our first day as a group was with our Drill Sergeant (DS). Drill Sergeant Huston was a gung-ho type of guy who had been given absolutely the worst job in the Army. He was responsible for the eighteen of us as we began our preparation to travel to parts unknown. DS Huston had been in charge of basic trainees, which involved soldiers who first come into the service and basically don't know the difference between "come here from sick-em." He was now in charge of a group of individuals that included Specialists, Captains, Majors, Lieutenant Colonels, and Colonels. Many of us had been in the service longer than he had been on Earth. One was in the Infantry Hall of Fame for his actions in Vietnam! We had people from all walks of life in this group; an individual running as a representative in his home state, a congressional aide, a retired police officer, an IRS auditor, a manager for Wal Mart, and a college professor. Basically all of us had the same two issues: We were completely surprised when called up and didn't have a clue where we were heading.

Drill Sergeant Huston had us get in a formation and marched

us about twenty yards, halted us, and gave the command, "File from the right, column right: March!" We looked at each other and sort of laughed, but we did what he said. After all, he was in charge, that day. The next day when he asked us to fall in, we protested.

"Not until someone tells us where we are going. Drill Sergeant, do you know where we are going?"

"Of course I do," was Drill Sergeant Huston's reply.

Finally, someone knew what was going on around here. I knew if anyone knew it would be a NCO. Our puzzle was about to be completed.

"Then where are we going drill sergeant?"

"Over there to get on a bus," was his reply, and he pointed to a location about forty yards away.

That was not what I meant, but a good drill sergeant is trained to answer the question that is asked of him. He answered my question. I was just not specific enough. I wanted to know if he knew where we were to be deployed. He thought I wanted to know where we were going to march. His response got a chuckle out of our group. We slowly started toward the bus and I replied, "Okay, we'll meet you over there!" We were not going to be treated like Privates. We already had an attitude; this was not helping. Besides, I felt like an idiot asking the question in the first place.

We looked at the training schedule and discovered we were about to begin basic training all over again. I went through basic training in January 1967, and was not quite prepared to become a private again. At first we thought this was a joke, but later found out CRC, like so many other government agencies, does not have a sense of humor.

One of the first exercises we conducted was low crawling with new privates in their first week of basic training. While it has been many years since basic training, I don't ever remember a group of senior officers coming to our low crawl pit and joining us on those types of maneuvers. I can only imagine what their letters sounded like when they wrote home. The low crawl with new troops was not something people with our rank and experience do. We had a combined total of almost three-hundred years military experience. We totally freaked out the privates that day. They asked us if we were part of "Delta Force." We just laughed and walked away. They knew they were in the presence of a "Special Group" of highly experienced soldiers.

The fact that I tripped and did a face plant in the low crawl pit while in their presence was not really a factor. They probably thought I was demonstrating a maneuver of how to get up, rush and recover to a protected position in a fire fight. They were impressed that such a high ranking individual would demonstrate such a maneuver. I don't think they even recognized my battle buddies doubled over in laughter as I spit sand and dirt from my mouth. It was embarrassing, but my low crawl and classy maneuvers were now complete.

We continued to work through the first week basic training requirements and presentations like, "The Role of the NCO," "The Role of the Officer," "Marking and Wearing of Clothes and Equipment." The final straw, however, was at the completion of the first week of basic training. We attended an orientation along with a group of basic training soldiers as a required class for all new soldiers. We were brought into a large auditorium that had approximately ten or more drill sergeants standing around like guards for a prison camp.

We sat in the back of the auditorium and were separated from approximately three-hundred plus basic training troops who were sleep deprived. No, they weren't being punished, but their life as they had known it in the civilian life world had changed about a week or two earlier. I can only imagine their anticipation and trouble sleeping in their new homes. They were sleepy, hoarse, and hacking up God only knows, and were about to receive a "Personal Affairs" class from one of the drill sergeants.

I did not take notes as to the presentation style. The errors were so obvious that they may be engrained into my brain forever. For example: The drill sergeant had a microphone to use but chose not to use it. He had a power point presentation that he had not reviewed carefully, and therefore was unfamiliar with its contents.

There were so many power point slides that the type of presentation he was about to give is commonly referred to as, "Death by Power Point." With his back to the troops, he read from the slides. Because he was not using a microphone, his voice could barely be heard at the back of the room. As a result, the privates were quickly falling asleep, only to be awakened by their drill sergeants with loud voices or sounds.

Other than that, it was one heck of a presentation.

However, those glaring issues were not the catalyst that caused us to uniformly get up and walk out of the presentation. What did make us leave were comments like, "Now don't go down to Columbus and buy a car at nineteen percent interest. You are what the car dealers are looking for!"

What? That is the same interest rate I received in basic training in 1967. I remember it well because I thought, "Heck, I don't want to be in the Army. I want to sell cars! That's a great interest rate for the seller."

If I wanted to buy a car down in Columbus, then I will go down and buy it. I understand the drill sergeants did not want the troops taken advantage of, but why was I listening to this. Besides, these troops won't be able to go to the Post Exchange (PX) without the drill sergeant being with them. Going downtown and purchasing a car would constitute a soldier being AWOL.

Next was a power point slide that stated, "No guns, knives, or black jacks in the barracks." That's a good thing and is important not to have those types of weapons handy in such an environment. That is not what upset me. What got my attention was his follow-up comment.

"No guns, knives, or black jacks in the barracks. We don't allow gambling during basic training."

What?

Gambling was a completely different slide but he was using the weapon "black jacks" to talk about gambling!

When the gambling statement was made, my battle buddies and I looked at each other and laughed out loud as to the comments. The drill sergeants continued their attention getting tactics to keep the soldiers awake and the drill sergeant on the speaking platform was oblivious to his work. I think in his mind he was killing them with his knowledge. He was killing them alright. They were dying of boredom! Other than that, it was one heck of a presentation.

That was it. I looked at our special group, and while I don't remember who initiated the departure, we all agreed, without any words of discussion, enough is enough, we were out of there, and we walked out, called CRC, and ordered vehicles back to pick us up and return us to the CRC site.

When we met with SFC Huston, we were more than a little upset. The training we had received thus far was completely inappropriate. It had been a waste of our time and our attitude was not one that someone wanted to address. Therefore, we vented our feelings to our drill sergeant. We were about to start in our second week, were still being asked by every presenter, "Where are you going?" to which our response was now, "We don't know, you tell us!"

We needed something more concrete and we were not getting it. This is where Drill Sergeant Huston stepped to the plate and basically trashed our training schedule. Huston was reprimanded, but a leadership principle that I remember from years ago was, "Always look out for the welfare of your personnel." We were his personnel and his responsibility, so he saw the need to take care of us, and he did.

DRILL SERGEANT HUSTON TAKES A HEAT ROUND FOR THE TEAM

There is a term in the military called "Minimal Essentials." That term represents the minimum tasks or objectives that must be completed for a successful mission. Collectively, we, along with Drill Sergeant Huston, developed a "Minimal Essentials" training schedule that would be beneficial for our personnel. Since we did not know where we were going, we thought a generic training process was in order. We identified the following essential elements for any mission:

1. First Aid: As far as I am concerned, first aid is an absolute must. I want everyone around me to know first aid, especially CPR. The age of some of us provided a great scenario for a potential heart attack. Also, if I get injured for some reason, I want every human being around me to know what to do. In addition to my own concerns, I want to be able to assist someone who might be injured while on a mission. Like so many of these minimal essential tasks, if you don't use it, you lose it. We needed all the refresher training they could give us on First Aid.

2. Radio Communications: Many of us had not used the proper format for radio communications in our civilian lives, so it was important that we be brought up to speed in that task. Radio frequencies, appropriate communications, calling in aircraft, artillery, and other common tasks are necessary in Radio Communications.

3. Weapons Qualifications/Familiarization: It was not just our basic weapon, but other weapons we might be exposed to in a combat zone was an important concept we needed to master. We needed to be familiar with weapons like the AK-47 before we arrived in whatever country we were going to. Entering a combat environment is not the time to ask, "How does this thing work?"

4. Map Reading: Need I say more? Men don't ask directions so we better be able to read a map! We were pretty sure there were few Holiday Inns and also certain that the prospect of stopping to ask directions to some town or location would not be in our best interest. While we did a significant amount of map reading training, it would have been

better to have used the actual maps in the country to which we were deploying. The problem with that option though, is we still did not know where we were deploying.

5. Physical Training: We laughed about it at first, but realized we had better take it seriously. We did some running, but we also did a significant amount of study concerning hydration and survival in a desert environment. If we are unable to physically perform on the battlefield, then we are of no use to anyone and can significantly hamper the mission. One issue we never considered in our physical training, however, was altitude. That proved to be a problem for long range activities later in our tour.

Added to the list was general study of both Iraq and Afghanistan. We studied the culture, dress, language, religion, politics, etc. Now, if only someone had told this "Special Group" where we were going, we would have been happy campers.

I keep referring to our group as a "Special Group." It should be noted that after many conversations with each other, we felt, for our own identification, we should have a "special name." We were getting tired of being called the "Special Group." CRC slipped up on one occasion and called us "Causality Replacements," which generated a significant bit of excitement in our group.

"What do you mean causality replacements? Where are we going?"

"Oh sir, I meant causality fillers," was the reply from the officer visiting with us.

"It means the same thing, you idiot!" was my reply. I was getting a little edgy because they knew something and were not telling us. We had to have a name.

We wanted to have something that people would remember, but it seemed all the cool names were taken, and besides, we weren't that cool. The official name of our group came by accident.

One evening, Colonel Gary Bass, Colonel Carl Turner, and

I were eating dinner in the mess hall when a young female NCO came over to our table and asked each one of us how many years we had served in the military. While we did not know who she was, we answered as professionally as we were able. Colonel Turner had completed twenty-eight years in the Army, Colonel Bass had thirty-four years, and I had completed thirty-seven years. The young NCO carefully wrote down the numbers and added them up. Her calculations gave her ninety-nine years total with the three of us. With that calculation, she turned to her fellow NCO at a separate table and said, "You owe me five dollars! I told you their total time in service was not over one hundred years!" That got quite a laugh from the soldiers in the mess hall, including the three of us. While not old, we had begun to refer to ourselves as "chronologically gifted." She was lucky; had she asked one of the other Colonels, then she would have lost, for Colonel Turner was the youngest of all the senior officers present.

I think that incident had something to do with the design and logo that came out a few days later. Sergeant Kevin Harshman, nicknamed "Harshdaddy," with the help of Sergeant Tim Batten, posted on our bulletin board the new group name: "Team Has Been." Our motto was: "We Answered the Call." It had a drawing that Harshdaddy drew of an Eagle with sweat popping from his forehead while he was trying to fly with a band aid on his wing, boxer (not briefs) type shorts on, and in one talon, a six-pack of beer, and in the other talon, a group of porn magazines. We loved the drawing, but I asked Harshdaddy if he would change the porn material to a remote control that might reflect our age group. Harshdaddy made the change, and shortly after arriving to our final destination, I had that drawing made into patches and t-shirts for everyone to wear. The patches, along with the t-shirts, became very popular with the soldiers in Afghanistan.

TIME TO SEPARATE THE MEN (NCOS) FROM THE BOYS (OFFICERS)

It took two weeks to complete our training; we decided it was time for "Team Has Been" to have a brief celebration. It was the right thing to do. We were going to be separated from our NCO Has Been members for at least two weeks, so we might as well party.

Lieutenant Colonel Craig Gilbert produced a bottle of smooth whiskey and some good cigars for us to smoke, and we let down what little hair we had. That's about it. Drinking good whiskey and smoking cigars. We were too tired and sore to go anywhere. After a night of heavy partying, we settled into bed to prepare for what was next. I think it was around 9:30 p.m.

We would be broken into two groups for the next phase of training. The NCOs were to stay at CRC and attend "Low Intensity Conflict" training with house-to-house clearing of obstacles, coordinated by SFC Huston. The officers would go to the Infantry School where we were to attend an "Officer Refresher Course." At last, we were going to receive some significant training for an objective that was still unknown to us.

We arrived at the Infantry School, and the introduction went something like this: "Welcome to the Ft. Benning Infantry School. We have a refresher course for officers here at the Infantry School. This course is designed for majors and below. We do not have anything planned for Lieutenant Colonels and Colonels. Basically, we have no idea what to do with you."

By this time, however, we had pretty much become independent and informed the Infantry School Staff of our issues and concerns. To the credit of the Infantry School and its staff, they bent over backwards to provide us with whatever we needed or at least thought we needed.

Since we still did not know where we were going, we started studying the cultural issues in both Afghanistan and Iraq. We also wanted to know about the Improvised Explosive Devices (IED's) that we had heard about. How were they made? How do we recognize them? How do we disarm them?

Uniforms were also a situation we were concerned about. Normally an officer buys his/her own uniform. However, we were issued uniforms and were told not to lose them or we would have to pay for their loss.

The uniforms did not quite match up. We had desert camouflage uniforms with jungle camouflage overcoats. We laughed that if we were in the middle of the desert, the bad guys would only have to shoot at the shrubbery that was out there and we would be wiped out!

After a week or so at the Infantry School, I returned to CRC in an effort to check our status for deployment. I visited briefly with a young Staff Sergeant and asked her if she had heard anything concerning our destination and departure. Her response was, "Yes sir, I know where you are going, but I am waiting for someone of higher authority to give me the okay to pass that along to you." I looked at her, then looked at my eagles, and lost what little bit of professionalism I had been able to maintain while there.

"Sergeant, there is only one person on this base that outranks me and that is the Commanding General of Ft. Benning! He is a Brigadier General! Is he going to come down here and tell me where I am going? I don't think so!" I screamed.

About five seconds elapsed between my comments and the Company Commander walking in. He was a young Captain who could see his life was about to change within the next ninety seconds. I walked into his office and slammed the door behind me and began what some might call a "foot locker counseling session" with the young Captain.

"Sir, I have a meeting in five minutes!"

"No problem Captain, when I get finished, you will have four minutes and some change to make that meeting." When I informed him of the comments I had received from the Sergeant, he indicated that I should check with the Operations Officer of the battalion for the assignments.

"Is he going to this meeting?"

"No, sir."

"See, you have four minutes and forty-five seconds to get to your meeting. Now that didn't take long did it?"

Fortunately, the Operations officer, a young Major, was about a five minute walk from the Company Commander's office, so I had the opportunity to cool down a bit.

I walked into the Operations Office and a Sergeant First Class was sitting at the front desk. "Sir, can I help you?"

"No Sergeant, you can't!" was my reply and I walked into the Major's office.

"Major, close your back door and lock it." I closed his front door and locked it. "I understand you know where we are being deployed."

"Yes sir, I have known that for about three weeks now."

There was a brief moment of silence. Actually I was at a loss of words for the second time in less than thirty minutes. For me, that had never happened before.

I just shook my head and said, "Why weren't we told?"

"Sir, I was informed that training was going great."

Now look at those last two statements: I asked the wrong question. I should have said, "Major, how's training going?"

Being the person to recognize a mistake, I rephrased the question somewhere around the following comment: "I'm sorry major, let me rephrase the question. Why weren't we told?"

At this point my mind went blank and I don't remember his response. I asked for my assignment information, and we slipped into another room. After providing him with my social security number, I found that I was going to be in Bagram, Afghanistan, as "Chief, Plan and Design ANA." I was clueless as to what that meant, but at least I knew where I was going.

"Is this going to be our little secret or can the rest of 'Team Has Been' find out where they are going?"

"No problem, sir, just have the soldiers come by, give me their social security numbers and I will let them know their assignment and destination."

"That is the wrong answer, Major! I have their security numbers in my folder. Here they are. I'll wait."

A few minutes later I finally found out where we were going. We all found out later that just because we were given a specific assignment, we did not necessarily get that job when we arrived in country. But at least we knew what country we were going to.

I got all the information to one of the Team Has Been members and the assignments were passed out to everyone. We were going as a group to Afghanistan. Now we could concentrate on training for a mission. It was vital we worked to learn as much about the culture and situation over there, so we would be fully prepared for our assignments. We would be there for one year, so it was extremely important that we took the remaining time allotted to learn as much as possible. Two days later we deployed!

Before I deployed, I was able to contact my receiving unit and visited with Lieutenant Colonel Bushy. I asked who I would be replacing and if there would be a hand-off time. I was informed there was no one to replace, and this was a new position. The position, Chief, Plan and Design ANA, meant I would be planning and designing an Army. The ANA stood for Afghan National Army. Great, I get to build an Army in a country that I have never been to, with people I did not know, in a language I did not speak, and with customs I did not understand. I was going in unprepared for what could be the most significant mission of my military career.

Good job preparing me CRC and Ft. Benning!

WELCOME TO THE END OF THE WORLD!

Our trip to Afghanistan was uneventful. In fact, it was not too bad. We were to depart at midnight from Ft. Benning, Georgia, for Atlanta Airport, but got away around four o'clock in the morning. We were already out of beer, had terrific hangovers, and were not even off the base!

We got to Atlanta and had a nice flight to Baltimore with a layover of three hours or so before departing to Frankfurt, Germany, for our next leg. In Baltimore they had a VIP lounge set up for "06s and above," which was very nice. The only down side was that some of the members of Team Has Been did not qualify to go to the VIP lounge, so we colonels tried to have a drink for them while we waited for our flight. Thus came hangover number two.

As we boarded the airplane, I must admit my mind was running wild as to what we had gotten ourselves into. Everyone tried to put on a positive persona, but it was obvious none of us had a clue as to what we could expect. I tried to sleep as much as I could in hopes I would wake up and find out I had been in one of the worst nightmares of my life. That did not happen. I was leaving the good old USA for what was to be the most significant mission in my entire military career.

Having not traveled as a VIP before, I was not familiar with the process of how to retrieve my baggage. My thoughts were to go to a location where our entire luggage would be stationed, find my duffle bags, and then proceed to our rooms either by car or by foot. As we deplaned in Frankfurt, I moved along with the rest of the troops to the staging area where our luggage was to be off loaded. After a significant amount of time, I came to the conclusion that my duffle bags had been lost in the move. I frantically started looking for my luggage. I was not aware that my luggage had been off loaded in a "Special Place" where VIPs could pick it up and not have to drag it around. Nice option. I just wish someone had informed me before I threatened that young Noncommissioned Officer about stealing my equipment. To this day, he is probably telling his friends about the "dork" Colonel that lost his luggage.

We got settled in at the 64th Replacement Detachment by Rhein-Main Air Base and began a four day wait for travel to Afghanistan. At this point of the trip, some of our guys were introduced to karaoke. It should be noted that karaoke has been banned in Germany because of one crazy night at the club! If it actually hasn't, then it should be. Envision this: ten guys all trying to sing, "Play That Funky Music White Boy," or something like that. Actually, I think it was "Born to be Wild," but it sounded like the "Play That Funky Music" piece.

I will have to admit that I actually did not participate in this event. I was only told later about the situation. I was off meditating as to what I could do to learn more about my mission. Actually, I was lost on the base and was trying to find my way back to the barracks.

For the next couple of days we made countless trips from the barracks to the Passenger Terminal (PAX) trying to determine our status for departure to Afghanistan. We also got to meet Sergeant Batten's wife, who was stationed in Germany right there in Rhein-Main. That was a bonus that he sure took advantage of. I think every Team Has Been member was excited to see him be with his wife.

After a couple of days of bugging the PAX staff, we were told to go back to the barracks because there was no way we would depart the next day, and to just stop hanging around. It was the basic, "Leave us the hell alone" speech. That worked for us.

With that bit of intelligence, four of the Team Has Been members decided to go on a trip on the Rhine River. Also, we told Sergeant Batten to go be with his wife because we were not going anywhere. I don't think he heard the last part of the message though. As soon as he heard, "be with your wife," he disappeared.

About 5:00 a.m. (0500 hrs) the next morning, I was awakened and told we had been scheduled and to get everyone up and ready to depart. We informed the PAX staff that we were busy and had other plans and to send someone else in our place. The PAX staff was pretty upset with us, but we reminded them of the conversation the previous day that included no transportation for us; then they changed the situation and we had a plane to catch all of a sudden.

We had gotten tired of the misinformation that had been given to us beginning at Ft. Benning and all the way to Frankfurt, so this change of status was not new. We already had an attitude that was not fun to be around, and it was getting worse. One of the Colonels said, "What if we don't go. Are you going to send us home?" Besides, we didn't have a clue as to where Sergeant Batten was.

We informed them to put another group on the plane in our place and we would catch the next one available. The PAX reluctantly agreed, and we departed on our journeys as planned. That gave Sergeant Batten more time with his family.

We had a blast traveling to St. Goar and having a fine German meal and some great wine. The weather was as gorgeous as anyone could have imagined. We tried our best to look at that trip as a fringe benefit because of what we were actually going to be doing for the next year. Take advantage of the opportunities when you can, because it may be your last time to do something like that.

Everyone, including Sergeant Batten, returned to the base the following day and prepared for the next flight out. I think our reaction the previous day got us moved up to a higher priority. The PAX personnel wanted to get rid of us as soon as possible. I guess they thought we might become trouble for the other troops. That actually never crossed our minds.

Our aircraft was to depart for Bagram, Afghanistan. Of course, we did not take a direct flight. We first landed in Uzbekistan, where we were introduced to our first little street vender, selling old money from Iraq. It was worthless, but we bought it anyway. Even though we weren't going to Iraq, it still made a nice souvenir. We had to wait for about four hours, and then departed for Kyrgyzstan and Manas Air Force Base. We were at Manas for a couple of days and received in-country briefings about Afghanistan. We received more information during those two days than we did during our entire time at CRC, Ft. Benning.

Our departure from Manas was quite a ride. We were loaded, cattle-car style, on a C-130 for a five hour flight to Bagram, our final destination. Fortunately, no one on our flight got sick during this portion of the trip, although it was less than smooth. It was during this particular flight that we experienced what was referred to as a "Combat descent and landing." We descended from our cruising altitude very quickly, released flares to thwart any heat-seeking missiles, and with a short final approach, found ourselves on the ground at Bagram Air Base. We were told the reason for such a descent was to provide a smaller target for the opposing forces to shoot us down.

THIS IS NOT A DREAM. THIS IS REALITY

Bagram Air Base, located in the Parvan Province, was initially the staging area for the 1980s Soviet invasion and occupation of Afghanistan. It has a 10,000 foot runway and is ideal for landing large aircraft. Bagram is located approximately forty-five miles north of Kabul, the capital of Afghanistan, and is strategically located for rapid deployment to the central and northern portion of this country.

Many of us thought, or hoped, Bagram Air Base would be our final destination, but we were informed shortly after our arrival that we would be dispersed to Kabul, the capital of Afghanistan. Most of us would be assigned to the Office of Military Cooperation—Afghanistan (OMC-A). I contacted Lieutenant Colonel Bushy concerning transportation and was informed we should have a convoy in a day or so. Sit and wait became the norm for us while at Bagram. We visited the Base Exchange (BX) and stocked up on reading material and food for the duration of our stay at this particular site.

After a couple of days at Bagram, we met the convoy that was assigned to pick us up and return to Kabul. It would be our first trip outside the airbase, and a familiar statement came to mind shortly after leaving the security of the airbase. "It's not the end of the world, but you can see it from there." I thought I was seeing the end of the world, at least as I knew it. At this particular time, I was not aware just how much this initial view would affect me for the rest of my life.

I had seen poverty in America. However, it was nothing compared to what I was observing just outside the gates and security of Bagram Airbase. Not only could I see the end of the world, but I was about to become a part of it and it was just my first day. I simply rode in my convoy vehicle with my mouth open, totally shocked as to what I was observing. I could not believe people lived in these conditions. The looks on their faces were not very inviting either. It appeared that at any minute we would be attacked by some disgruntled civilians.

Approximately half way back to Kabul, we lost three of our

five-vehicle convoy due to mechanical issues. Vehicle number three had a flat, so four and five stopped to assist. We did not know that because the convoy commander had forgotten to bring radios. Vehicle one was traveling at a high rate of speed and was leaving my vehicle (two) behind, and almost out of sight. To add to the problem, our vehicle was having problems with its power and was only able to travel at a less than average speed. Radios were to be in place and communication tested before departure, and the distance between convoy vehicles were to be predetermined before departure. They were to be close enough for safety and security, but not so close that one IED could destroy two or more in one blast. In this case, our five vehicles had about a five mile separation between vehicle one and vehicle five.

For some unknown reason, vehicle one eventually looked back and noticed the four remaining vehicles were nowhere to be seen. The driver of vehicle one turned around to return to us and see what the problem was. At that point, all we knew was that we could not keep up with the lead vehicle and did not have a clue as to where the remaining three vehicles were. The convoy commander told us to continue toward Kabul and he would go back to check on the others. While we were new in the country, we were educated enough to know that this was not good convoy management. We refused to move forward and turned with the lead vehicle to head back and check on the others.

When we got back to the other vehicles, we observed a crowd of people beginning to gather. It was decided we would set up a defensive perimeter for protection. We had limited ammunition, but felt it would be adequate to protect ourselves. We were able to borrow enough 9mm rounds to have two clips per person. However, it was only the Team Has Been members who had acquired the additional ammunition. The convoy security also had rounds, but they would not share. We had some Air Force personnel in our convoy, but they had absolutely no ammunition.

Our particular vehicle had a female Air Force major on board without ammo, so I handed her one of my clips for her 9mm. I said,

"It's time to cowgirl up and establish our perimeter." She looked at me like I had lost my mind. We dismounted the vehicles, and when I came around behind ours, the female major was standing there with the clip I had given her earlier. She either did not know how to load the clip or was unwilling to do so. She handed it back to me.

At this moment, my thoughts of having women in combat started to collide with my values development as a child and adolescence. My father had raised me to be a protector of others, especially of those that could not protect themselves. It was, however, the first time I had to exercise that option and I have to admit that I was thinking, "If something goes wrong and we have a firefight of some type, this woman is going to get me killed, because I have now become more concerned about protecting her than the team." I told her to stay near me while the flat was being changed. I don't remember that individual's name, but I lost a lot of respect for her because of her actions during that incident. She ended up at OMC-A but we rarely talked during her short stay there. Fortunately, we were able to get the tire changed and move on to Kabul without incident.

IN-PROCESSING AND MY NEW HOME

Upon arrival at OMC-A, we were welcomed by Lieutenant Colonel Bushy and his team. As mentioned earlier, I had been in contact with Lieutenant Colonel Bushy while in Ft. Benning, and he assured me that everything was beautiful at Kabul and they even had roses growing in the compound. He wasn't kidding. They actually had roses and other flowers in bloom there. They tried to make it as comfortable as possible. Lieutenant Colonel Bushy was as smooth a transition personnel officer as I had ever seen. I very much enjoyed getting to know him and work with his staff. At least for me, he had a very calming presence about him that, at that particular time in my life, I needed.

Part of our processing was to get our housing for our duration while in Afghanistan. I was assigned to the "Moon House." I have no idea how the various houses got their names. It was probably just an arbitrary name given when OMC-A was established. Each of the houses had similar names. We were next door to the "Sun House."

These houses were located off base from OMC-A; however, they were fairly close to the base headquarters. An Afghan driver would run a shuttle each morning and evening to pick us up and deliver us back to our respective houses. We got to know the drivers pretty well. I gave one driver a Russian nickname, "Peekupndropoff." Fortunately, he saw the humor in the nickname.

Still, traveling to and from the residence was a little uneasy for me the first few weeks. We were told to ride in the back seat, and if the driver made any deviation from the route, we were to ask him to get back on the route immediately. If he did not do that, we were to stick our 9mm pistol or rifle to the back of his head and repeat our command. It was said that during the Russian Occupation, a Russian commander's driver of four years went left instead of right one day, took the commander outside of town, and executed him. That certainly got my attention. However, we did not have any such problems.

I eventually got used to the travel and began to bond with a great group of guys at the Moon House. We had Army, Navy, Air Force, Marine, and Seabees there and they really enjoyed ribbing each other and even themselves. They were a tight group and friendships from that environment will not soon be forgotten. It was a great representation of working across the services. When they came into the "Moon House" they were all equals and friends.

I fondly remember meeting this one Air Force major who was dressed in a traditional Afghan outfit. He was wearing what many refer to as a Massoud Hat. The Massoud Hat looks almost like a strange head of hair on someone. I said, "Man, who is your barber? I want a haircut like that!" He looked at me without cracking a smile and removed his hat. I thought it was funny, but I was quickly getting the impression that the humor was not as infectious as I had hoped. There was a moment of silence (I think about three years worth), and then he started laughing. I knew then that I was in a room of professional jokesters, and this environment might be just what I needed. I also found out quickly that if you didn't have a sense of humor, you were fresh meat for everyone in the house. They could feed on you like sharks. I loved it!

Back at OMC-A, we went through the basic processing and got a tour of the compound. We were shown where the medical station was located, where to go for meals, laundry, PX, workout facilities, and religious gatherings. My initial assignment of the Plan and Design of the Afghan National Army had been changed. While I was assigned to OMC-A, my slot had been taken by another Colonel. I would be finding out later my specific assignment. Meanwhile, I was to continue my in-processing until I had an opportunity to meet with the Chief of OMC-A, Major General Craig Weston.

There were eighteen original members of "Team Has Been" that met and formed at Ft. Benning. While most of us were in the Kabul area and more specifically with OMC-A, there were others who were assigned to sites around Afghanistan. For example, Captain Jerry Simpson was sent south to Kandahar as part of security for that region. He was definitely in his element, as Captain Simpson was a Trooper for the state of Texas and loved his work. I pretty much lost contact with Jerry during his tenure in Kandahar. I was, however, able to hear some news about him through a former Operations Officer also deployed in that area. You know, Walt Disney said it best, "It's a small world after all!" Major Doug Long had been my operations officer in Shawnee, Oklahoma when I was a battalion commander. He, too, had been called to active duty and was assigned to the Kandahar region. He worked with Captain Simpson during his deployment.

Back at OMC-A, many of our junior noncommissioned officers (NCO's) were assigned as security details in and around the compound. They would also be shooters in convoys that were being used to travel around the country and, especially, back and forth to Bagram, which was the pick-up and drop-off location of personnel who would be transitioning to and from the country.

Most of them were not too thrilled with those options, but at least they had a job identified and knew what their mission was.

ASSIGNMENT CHANGE

As I mentioned earlier, my assignment of "Chief, Plan and Design ANA" had been given to another Colonel. His name was Colonel Laurent (Bake) Baker, a Marine Colonel who was full of spit and vinegar. I was told to shadow him for the next couple of weeks until they decided what to do with me.

I was upset by that arrangement and let it be known that I had a suggestion as to what they could do with me. Since my job had been filled, they could send me home. My life and marriage, as I knew it, had been ruined and I would never be the same because of this deployment. My reflection on this deployment was half right. I will never be the same because of this deployment; I will be better, and my life and marriage were not ruined. They are actually better; I didn't think that was possible. God works in mysterious ways, and this was just one example. However, I was not aware of the changes in my life that were happening at that particular moment in time.

I quickly discovered that Colonel Baker knew his business. Of all the people I met during my deployment, he impressed me the most. Colonel Baker was in charge of the Defense Operation Sector (DOS) and everything that happened at OMC-A went through his office. It was at this time I found out exactly what the responsibility was with the title.

Colonel Baker was responsible for building and designing the Afghan National Army. This was from the ground up. It was an impossible mission to accomplish, so they got a marine to do it. Colonel Baker was a genius at working with people, and knew how to push the right buttons and when.

His assignment was a home run call by the Chief, OMC-A. Colonel Baker did more to keep up morale and motivation for the troops that were assigned to him than anyone on the base.

He was a coach, teacher, cheerleader, disciplinarian, counselor, and anything else that was needed to accomplish the mission. I understand he is in Washington, D.C. now at the Pentagon. I hope I will read some day that he made General.

The Chief of OMC-A was Major General Craig Weston. He was an Air Force Academy graduate and in the field of acquisitions. I admit I was never really comfortable around him, nor did I like some of his decisions. However, I don't think he was there to work for my approval. I will say that every decision he made had the soldiers in mind, and especially the junior NCOs and officers. He was mission-driven and a "soldier's first" type of chief.

I remember specifically during the Christmas time, a memorandum was sent indicating no senior officers or NCOs would be allowed to go home during the Christmas holiday. That time would be reserved for junior NCOs and officers, and in that group, those who had small children would have a higher priority. The selfish side of me was upset, but had I been in the chair he was in, I would like to think I would have done the same thing. Major General Weston certainly looked beyond himself and took care of his troops. He was a very intelligent person, and I hold him personally responsible for much of the news not getting out to the US papers.

That sounds like a very negative statement to say, but it is actually a compliment. Our civilian newspapers tend to only report the negative of what is going on in Afghanistan and Iraq. If something good happens, it gets very little publicity. We send that information out through our Public Affairs Office, but it's the newspapers that decide what is printed and what is not. I don't necessarily hold the newspapers responsible for this either. I lay the blame on our society that seems to want to read the negative side of the stories that happen around the world. Bad news sells.

The reason you didn't hear a lot from Afghanistan was because of people like Major General Weston. His record of successes was unbelievable. Hospitals built, recruiting stations established, Afghanistan National Army battalions (Kandaks) stood up, security forces stabilized, presidential election a major success, goodwill established all over the country between the Afghans and American forces, just to name a few. He also gave the final approval to build the National Military Academy of Afghanistan, but he never got to see the grand opening because he rotated back to the United States and entered retirement from the Air Force. I know he had many successes in his life, but I think it would be hard to top his last assignment.

I have always wanted to thank Major General Weston for letting me be a small part of his career.

HOW DID WE GET THERE IN THE FIRST PLACE

Afghanistan has an interesting history that many people may not realize. It is formally called the *Islamic Republic of Afghanistan,* and is located in Southern Asia, north and west of Pakistan and east of Iran. It has approximately the same amount of square miles as Texas. Alexander the Great traveled through Afghanistan in his sojourns to India. In the 700's, Islamic conquers took over the country. In the 1300's Genghis Khan invaded and conquered the country.

As you read about the years of development and redevelopment of Afghanistan, one thing that is systemic: they are familiar with war and have proven to be fighters beyond reproach.

We need only to look at the recent history of Afghanistan to find their involvement with serious conflict since the 1970's. The conflicts were launched by foreign adversaries as well as their own civil wars.

The invasion of Russia, in 1979, began in the Hindu Kush mountain area. The Russians were supposedly attempting to stop the spread of Islamic Fundamentalism. However, the Soviets were not prepared for the type of hit and run war that was very familiar to the Afghans. The Russians were strong in number, with the involvement of eighteen hundred T-62 tanks and eighty thousand troops from the fortieth Army. The troop strength eventually grew to more than one hundred and fifty thousand as they became more committed to their efforts. There were also more than two thousand armored personnel vehicles to add to the chaos that was to ensue.

The Afghan rebels, also known as the "mujahedeen," were disenchanted because the new Afghan regime was relying on significant intervention and support from a foreign country. That caused unrest throughout the country because of the concern the regime was selling out their country to Russia. Does that sound familiar?

The United States, as well as other countries, initially ignored the Russian invasion, because it was not really clear why they were in Afghanistan to begin with. Many Afghans had been educated in Russia and spoke the language, so the invasion did not appear to be a threat to anyone, even the Afghans.

In 1986, the United States had its own problem with the Iran Contra Affair. This scandal was front page on our news reports, so Afghanistan was basically shoved into the background. We were more concerned with how the media was portraying the Reagan administration and what might come from these hearings that were being conducted.

Meanwhile, the United States was funneling support to Afghanistan to help the mujahedeen with their fight against the Russians. The weapons the Afghans had were no match for the heavier armed MI-24 attack helicopter that had been recently introduced in the war. The support from the United States helped purchase the Stinger Missile that would eventually turn the tide is the Afghan/Russian conflict. The United States involvement in the Afghan/Russian Affair was a covert operation for the United States, just like the Iran/Contra Affair. We were just more covert about it!

In February 1989, after almost 14,000 casualties, the Russians departed through the northern plains of Afghanistan, leaving behind millions of mines that had been scattered through out the ten year conflict. While they did supposedly leave maps, many of the mines could not be detected with electronic devices. Therefore, they had to be individually probed and destroyed. During 2004–2005, reports indicated approximately three hundred Afghans were killed or seriously injured monthly by undetected mines. According to the Major General Sharif, over eighteen hundred mines were extracted and destroyed at the site where we built the National Military Academy of Afghanistan.

With the Russians out of Afghanistan, the tribal factions took to fighting each other. While Ahmad Shah Massoud was a major factor in the elimination of the Russians and in rallying the mujahedeen to fight, he was not loved by all people. Regional warlords postured for positions of power and significant battles resulted in this civil war. Former President Ronald Reagan tagged the mujahedeen as "Freedom Fighters," but it was basically a matter of chaos as each tribal leader tried to gain control over various territories.

A group of warriors that saw limited action during the Afghan/Russian war was called the "Afghan Arabs." Many were not Afghan, nor Arabs; however, they were much revered as fighters in the Muslim world. As the Soviet conflict began to wear down, the "Afghan Arabs" took on other jihad issues, such as Bosnia. The primary leader that emerged from the "Afghan Arab" soldiers was Osama bin Laden, who was from Saudi Arabia. Bin Laden came from a wealthy family and he used his wealth and influence to funnel money, weapons, and additional "Afghan Arabs" into Afghanistan.

Around 1995, a village mullah established, with the help of Pakistan, a new armed movement called the Taliban, which means "Students of Islam;" in 1996, they confronted the mujahedeen.

The Taliban basically broke apart what little continuity the muja-hedeen had and from 1996 until 2001 was in control of most of Afghanistan.

The Taliban was headed by Mullah Mohammad Omar, and, while in power, he enforced the "Sharia Law" to the extreme. The Sharia is based on the Qur'an and addresses issues such as economics, business, contracts, sexuality, hygiene, and politics. The Taliban were also extremely cruel to women. Public flogging and executions were not uncommon for women by the Taliban. They were also denied education and medical treatment from male doctors unless accompanied by a male. They wore burqas so as to not corrupt men not related to them. It appears the primary issue with the Taliban was consistency. If you violated one of their laws, you were punished severely.

Two individuals I became very close to need to be recognized here. They are true heroes of mine and today I consider them my brothers.

Dr. Sardar Sherzad was my translator, and Major General Mohammad Sharif became the Superintendent/Commandant of the National Military Academy of Afghanistan and a very close and dear friend. Dr. Sardar had lived as a young boy during the Taliban regime and MG Sharif had been educated in Russia, later fought against the Russians, and then joined the United Islamic Front for the Salvation of Afghanistan, also known as the Northern Alliance, as one of their commanders to combat the Taliban.

I asked Dr. Sardar to share with me his feelings about the Taliban and their work in the country during his time as a young man. Below is an article he wrote, just as he wrote it. I sent this to my wife to share with her students in her classes in the U.S.

The Taliban were strict Muslims. They were trying to impose many situations on people. In the Taliban government in Afghanistan, people couldn't use their own rights. Men were not allowed to feel free and do as they wanted. They were not allowed to wear suits, to be bare headed, to have long and tidy hairs.

Young male students of Kabul University were supposed

to wear turbans, grow long beards, and wear national clothes. Women were not allowed to work at the offices. They were not allowed to go outside of home alone. They had to have a family member with themselves while walking out of home. They had to wear burqas and cover all parts of their body. If Taliban groups had some doubt about the man walking with the girl the couple would be stopped on the spot and were put under investigation individually. Taliban asked the boy the names of girl's parents and relatives and asked the girl vice versa.

If the information taken from both sides was similar, the couple was released, otherwise if it was not they were sent to jail.

If a girl's ankle was bare and people could watch that, they slashed her on the ankles and even sometimes picked such girls up and put them in jail.

Women were not allowed to talk to shop keepers while shopping in Bazaar. They had to have a man with them. Women were not allowed to use taxis alone. If they did the driver was given a punishment. The drivers were not allowed to pick up a woman alone.

All the schools were closed for girls. Small girl students were supposed to go to Islamic schools called Madrasa. These Madrasas were providing just Islamic instructions inside Mosques.

National buses were divided into two parts. Front gate of the bus was allocated for women and the rear one for men and there was a metal, wood, cloth wall in the middle of the bus to separate men from women.

Hospitals were divided similarly in the two parts. Male doctors were not allowed to treat female patients even if they died. Afghanistan rarely had female doctors in surgery, therefore, male surgeons were not allowed to operate on female patients. As the result those women who required surgical operations finally passed away.

There is much to say about the cruelty of Taliban on women and men in Afghanistan but the time doesn't allow me to continue. Finally I have to say that people of Afghanistan were very upset. They were hopeless. They did not even expect a bright future for Afghanistan.

Fortunately, we all feel free now and live in a free environment without any threat. We hope, we'll never repeat such an experience inside our country in the future.

Our women are all free now. They have their rights according to our new constitution. Our young girls go to schools. Women work in offices. They support their families and share the responsibilities with other family members.

Kabul University seems different than it was at that time. Girls and boys sit beside one another in one class studying. They walk together.

Totally, Afghanistan has changed a lot since the defeat of Taliban Government. We now have new hopes and new constitutions.

Much later, after I had established my ability to get things done and having been honored with the trust of Major General Sharif, I asked him specific questions relating to his experiences. Below are his responses. You might find some of the comments directed toward the Russians to resemble some of the thoughts al Qaeda has made toward the U.S. forces. It will be your decision to draw similar conclusions. I asked Major General Sharif the following questions:

General Sharif, when we first met, you told me that you were educated in Russia. Were many Afghans educated that way?

Before 1979, the Afghan government sent a limited number of Afghan students to Turkey, India, and the United States. After the aggression of the Russian forces to Afghanistan, the international community condemned the occupation of Afghanistan by Russian forces. The relations of western countries, especially NATO members, were cut with Afghanistan and they no longer accepted Afghan students for higher education. By that time, the Soviet Union started accepting Afghan students to their higher education centers free of charge. After that, based on Afghan government requirements, all Afghan officers were sent to Russia for higher education degrees.

When Russia first came into Afghanistan, was it considered a threat?

> Yes, the aggression of Russian forces in Afghanistan was a distinct threat for the country, based on the following reasons:
>
> Afghanistan was, is and will be an Islamic country and the Russians were identified as infidels. All Afghans have struggled against aggressors for getting their independence and freedom throughout our history. Therefore the invasion of Russian forces to Afghanistan was definitely considered as a threat to our national pride and freedom. Our two neighboring countries, Iran, where the Islamic revolution had seceded by that time and Pakistan, which was afraid of the Russian forces arrival to warm waters, felt the great threat. Based on the above reasons and the great support of the international community to the Afghanistan Mujahidin, the Russian forces were defeated in Afghanistan.

When did the Russians officially leave Afghanistan?

> After ten years of physical existence in Afghanistan, Russia quit the country on 15 February, 1989 based on the Geneva Agreement. That date is celebrated each year in Afghanistan.

Why were the religious factions fighting after the Russians left?

> After the Russians quit the country, the communist government frequently proposed to sign a peace treaty with the Afghan Mujahidin, which would finally lead to power transition to them, but unfortunately, due to the interferences of neighboring countries, which are still going on, the internal wars start inside the country after the Mujahidin officially got the power on 28 April 1991.

Was the Taliban initially seen as something that would stop the religious battles?

> Yes, the Taliban party was established out of the country just for ensuring security, stability, justice, and Sharia Law inside

the country. They entered the country through Spin Boldak and occupied Kandahar and Helmand. They were initially supported by the Islamic Government of Afghanistan because they had a positive perception of their work and mission.

Conclusion from MG Sharif:

> The time between 1979 and 2001 is considered as a black period in social, political, and economical life for Afghans. During this period all economical, cultural, and social infrastructures were devastated and millions of people were either killed, injured, or disabled. The economical resources were ruined. The doors to education and development were shut, and the historical statues like the Buddhas at Bamyan, which have been built in the sixth century, were destroyed. The Taliban declared the statues as idols which are forbidden under Sharia Law.
>
> Today (2004–2005), the Afghan people are hopeful. They all look forward to the continuation of coalition support led by the U.S. for achievement of more improvements in the country. During the last five years, there have been a lot of improvements in different areas such as education, higher education, construction, hospitals, road and highways construction, Afghanistan National Army (ANA), and Afghanistan National Police (ANP) reformation as well as training, communications, and the future of our country is looking bright.

While the Taliban were initially looked upon favorably because they could provide the consistency that was needed between the tribes or ethnic groups, they soon became terrorists in their own right because of their interpretation of the Sharia Law and religion. As MG Sharif indicated, it was a dark period for both the people and the country of Afghanistan during their rule.

OUR DAY OF INFAMY

We move ahead to our modern day version of the attack on Pearl Harbor. If you ask people of almost any age what happened on December 7, 1941 the response is generally the bombing of Pearl Harbor, or the day we were attacked by Japan. The attack on the Twin Towers on September 11, 2001 is today's version of Pearl Harbor. It was to today's youth and adults what December 7, 1941 was to our society at that time. Basically, our lives changed as we knew it and we haven't been the same since.

Through a coordinated attack, Islamic terrorists that were connected to al Qaeda attacked the United States on its home soil. The attack and style of this magnitude was almost impossible to believe. This had never happened before in the United States. We had a bombing at the twin towers a few years prior by a Middle Eastern terrorist and the bombing of the Alfred E. Murrah building in Oklahoma City, Oklahoma in April 1995. The Murrah bombing was thought to be a terrorist attack from a foreign country, but later it was discovered that the culprit was actually from the United States. But to hijack four commercial aircraft, fly two of them into the twin towers, one into the Pentagon, and the fourth one crash in a Pennsylvania countryside was not even in our wildest imaginations. You couldn't dream this up without having a Hollywood script!

I was in a colleague's office at the university where I taught and thought, "What the hell is happening here?" At that time only one plane had hit the twin towers. I was not exactly sure what was going on. As I was preparing to cross campus, I saw the second plane hit the towers and I immediately contacted my reserve unit where I was commander and told our full-time personnel to lock down and go to full alert. I would be there before the day was out. Within an hour, I received word to lock down the reserve center and stand by for additional communications.

I crossed campus to make a quick visit with our teacher candidates and, as I entered the building, I noticed the large crowd of people watching the events unfold on the jumbo screen in our technology building. Initially, I thought they were viewing the initial two attacks. I quickly realize the third hijacked plane had hit the Pentagon. The students were extremely concerned and rumors were flying as to what might happen next. Since I had a military background, I received many questions as to my thoughts. At this particular time, I was about as much in the dark as they were.

We found out shortly that a fourth aircraft crashed that was tracked as if it were heading to Washington D.C. Headed for the capitol maybe? We will never know. Fear and tension was beginning to mount across campus. The news reports were already speculating terrorists and that word automatically channeled thoughts to the Middle East. Profiling was already being generated by the news reports, our faculty, and our students.

I visited with the students and attempted, to the best of my ability, to put them at ease and not do or say something they might regret. They were extremely angry about what had just happened and wanted revenge on the masterminds of these tragic events. I told them more information would be forthcoming and to not jump to conclusions, like so many did with the Murrah bombing, and falsely accuse someone of a particular nationality before the evidence had been gathered. I don't think they really believed me, because I really didn't believe myself.

Only after I departed the university campus and started to Shawnee, Oklahoma, where I was the commander of a reserve unit, did I take the time to reflect over what was going on. Since I was not around during the bombing of Pearl Harbor, I reflected on another significant emotional event in my life. On November 22, 1963, John F. Kennedy was assassinated in Dallas, Texas, about an hour from my home. He was the first president that had been elected on television, lived openly in the White House on television, and died for real on television. He was the youngest president ever elected; the youth of that time had really jumped on his bandwagon.

Lee Harvey Oswald was captured shortly after in a Dallas

movie theater and was charged with the murder of our president, as well as the murder of J.D. Tippit, one of Dallas's police officers. That seemed to put our fears on hold, but only for a short period of time.

The following day, Jack Ruby was in the basement of the police station and assassinated Oswald in front of worldwide TV cameras. I was laying in my sister's living room and she was in the kitchen cooking something when this happened. I jumped up and shouted, "Someone just shot Lee Harvey Oswald." My sister ran into the room and started crying. She feared what was to happen next. She was almost hysterical.

While it was not to the level of the four hijacked aircraft and the events that followed, it was the first time for the world to see, live, events unfold that had been unscripted from beginning to the end. We just did not know where the end might be.

It was later published, in national tabloids, that Oswald was to kill Kennedy, Ruby was to kill Oswald, and there was a bounty on Ruby. If it came from the tabloids then it must be true. At least that is what a significant number of people who read them while waiting to check out of a supermarket think. Comments like that helped generate conspiracy theories that live today.

Conspiracy theories have also run amuck with the twin towers disasters. Fingers have been pointing at almost everyone imaginable except you and me, and I am not sure about you!

The only individual to step to the plate and take responsibility is Osama bin Laden and al Qaeda. In the Islamic extremist thinking, we are the infidels and should be destroyed. We are an immoral group of people that doesn't deserve to be on this earth. Jihad has been thrust upon us and we will not survive al Qaeda's wrath.

I arrived at my reserve center in the middle of the afternoon and the word had already come down from higher command that we lock down and be prepared for anything and everything. I had to prepare a statement for our soldiers about the possibilities, and the truth was, I actually did not know what the possibilities were. I decided that would be my statement. Doesn't sound like much of a leader, but this was not the time to make stuff up. I had to be honest with my troops.

The United States did not waste time getting involved with the terrorists cells. In October 2001 the Air Force sent an elite special operations team, along with CIA operatives, to coordinate air strikes on specific Taliban targets in what would be called "The Battle of Tora Bora." Tora Bora is southeast of Kabul and south of Jalabad near the Kyber Pass. That was a quick strike in attempt to disrupt and destroy Taliban cells and capture or kill bin Laden. Evidence was contradictory as to whether bin Laden was ever at Tora Bora at that time. However, it was the best intelligence the United States forces had.

Tora Bora was followed in early March by Operation Anaconda. It was suspected that bin Laden and other high ranking Taliban or al Qaeda leaders were in the Shah-i-Kot Valley located in the Paktia province in the southeastern portion of Afghanistan. Operation Anaconda was commanded by Major General Franklin Hagenback, who later became the Superintendent of West Point.

The basic result of Operation Anaconda was the removal of most of the Taliban and al Qaeda presence in the Shah-i-Kot Valley. The downside to the operation was still no bin Laden, nor any of his high-ranking lieutenants.

At this time, the United States was about to become involved in a long and methodic war on terrorism. That is a problem that I could see from the outset. It didn't appear that we had good or solid objectives. Yes, we were fighting the war on terrorism, but what were our objectives?

As former President George H. W. Bush said during Operation Desert Shield and Operation Desert Storm, "This will not be another Viet Nam." What did he mean by that? My students at the university did not seem to have a clue. I believe he meant this war will not be fought in Washington, but in the battlefield. We had specific objectives to reach, they were reached, and we pulled back. Remember George Bush, Sr. was criticized for not going in after Saddam Hussein. That was not part of the objective.

George had one of the highest ratings ever for a sitting president and eleven months later he was defeated by Bill Clinton. To go from the highest approval rating ever in a presidency to defeat in less than one year shows the impatience and short memory of our American society.

We were entering the war on terrorism in 2001, and initially the objectives seemed fairly clear. The primary objective was to get Osama bin Laden. Somehow though, we got Iraq into the mix and objectives got somewhat distorted. We started looking for "Weapons of Mass Destruction" (WMD) and that objective split our forces in such a manner that success on either front would be next to impossible.

I supported the decision of our President. However, there are a couple of issues that made me shutter. During a press briefing/interview, President Bush (Junior) was attempting to establish his defense of finding the "WMDs." Questioning was already beginning on the "why" we were even in Iraq. I don't remember the question/answer session so much as a statement that President Bush made toward the end of the interview, "After all, he did try to kill my daddy."

As soon as he made that statement, I thought to myself, "He is taking this personal, and we don't need to be going to that level."

Later, when President Bush landed on an aircraft carrier to the delight of millions, stepped up to the podium and announced victory and that the war was over, he briefly surpassed his father in the popularity polls. Then he had the highest approval rating ever for a sitting president. There is nowhere to go but down, correct? He left office with one of the lowest approval ratings ever for a sitting president. I would call that, "Going from the Penthouse to the Outhouse." The bottom line is we were there and I was called to active duty with a mission that was yet to be determined.

MISSION POSSIBLE,
WITH TWO EXCEPTIONS...

My first two weeks or so, I basically followed Colonel Baker around and was quietly telling myself that I was glad I didn't have the job that was initially assigned to me. I did not know what Major General Weston had in store for me, but as time passed, I began to find out from the other Colonels that Weston was, after interviewing each in great detail, offering them positions that not only fit their military field, but also their civilian specialties. I was getting positive feedback from the individuals being interviewed, but was a little concerned with just how my military expertise would fit in.

I started my own rumors, which is really not a healthy thing to do. When I let my imagination run wild, I usually get myself into all kinds of problems. Why should this be any different?

My most recent assignment that I thought would be of benefit to OMC-A was that of Inspector General. I had been the Deputy Inspector General with the 90th Regional Support Command in Little Rock, Arkansas a few years earlier, and that training was very valuable in this type of arena. An Inspector General works in three basic areas within the military: assistance, inspections, and investigations. The IG is the eyes and ears for the commanding general. The IG answers to no one other than the commander. However, I did not know if I would be working with OMC-A or the larger command there at the Kabul Compound.

Let me explain the difference between Kabul Compound and OMC-A. OMC-A was a part of a larger unit in the compound. Major Weston was not the commander of OMC-A. His title was Chief, OMC-A. There was a larger contingency within the perimeter of Kabul Compound. That consisted of the Central Command for Afghanistan. That was commanded by Lieutenant General David Barno, a West Point Graduate. General Barno answered directly to Central Command (CENTCOM) back in Tampa, Florida.

To say that the Kabul compound was a little top heavy with officers is an understatement. There were some people that did get lost in the shuffle. Some even took pride in that accomplishment. Personally, I think those that were lost were satisfied with that situation and had no one to blame but themselves. The commander at Task Force Phoenix, Brigadier General Thomas Mancino said it so eloquently, "You can't sling a dead cat around your head here without hitting a Colonel!"

"Yes, sir, General, you are correct!" I was the last of the Colonels from "Team Has Been" to meet with Major General Weston, and wondered exactly how I would fit into the organization. The Inspector General option came up only briefly and then went by the wayside. *How in the world will he be able to fit me into a meaningful role for the next year?* With much anticipation, I entered his office, rendered a salute with the response, "Sir, Colonel James Wilhite, reporting as ordered." My life was about to make another change that I was not expecting.

Major General Weston was very pleasant in our initial visit. He welcomed me to the family of OMC-A and we talked about family experiences and about the IRR reserve call-up situation. While he wanted to know what I had to bring to the table, I believe he had already made up his mind for my tenure in Afghanistan. Like a pro, however, he presented it to me in such a manner that I would have been a fool not to take it.

Major General Weston began by saying, "I see from your military biography you have extensive work in and around the university arena."

"Yes sir, I have spent most of my career in the education ranks and was a Professor of Education when I was called to active duty."

"You have been a professor, administrator, Board of Examiner for Colleges and Universities; you have served on many committees relating to university accreditation and the like."

"Yes, sir, I have." At this point I had no idea where he was heading.

"Your biography also states you have worked as a Military Admissions Liaison Officer (MALO) for West Point, so you must be familiar with its organization and function."

"Yes, sir, that is an extremely rewarding job. I get to meet the best and brightest students in the nation."

"Well Jim, I have a mission here that would really fit your civilian expertise, if you choose to accept it."

Wow, I get a choice to accept it or not! I did not say that to him out loud, but that is what was going through my mind. Also what was going through my mind was, "If I don't accept this assignment, I may not have a choice as to the next one."

Major General Weston continued, "We have a plan here to develop and implement a university for Afghanistan students that will be the future of this country. We want to build it using the model of the United States Military Academy at West Point. Having reviewed your biography, and based on our conversation, I would like for you to consider heading up that project as its team chief."

"Yes, sir, I would love to take that challenge!"

"I have two individuals that I want you to talk to. They must approve of you before we can move forward with this mission. They are here from West Point."

I consider myself a people person, and thought the interview would be a piece of cake. Major General Weston said one was an electrical engineer and head of that department and the other was a lawyer that taught at West Point.

Great I have to visit with a couple of guys that probably don't have a funny bone in their body. I may not like the taste of this cake.

Colonel Barry Shoop and Lieutenant Colonel David Wallace stood between me and my dream mission. I was going to have to convince them that I could handle the situation and work toward mission accomplishment.

There was a slight problem though. They knew something that I didn't, and that was just how long they were going to be there. That jumped up and slapped me right in the face a few weeks later.

Outside our mess hall was a seating area where many soldiers ate during their meal time. This is where I met Colonel Shoop and Lieutenant Colonel Wallace. We shared a cool drink together and instantly developed a great rapport and friendship. They filled me in on what had been happening prior to my/our arrival and how the study had been put together by previous West Point personnel. They were not the first pair over there, nor would they be the last group to arrive.

A team had arrived earlier to determine if such an academy was even feasible. The previous team had recommended beginning the development stages of an academy for Afghan students. They had also recommended the possibility of having Afghan students compete for a slot to attend the United States Military Academy at West Point. The interviews for the selection of an Afghan student had been completed and final selection had been made. It was now up to Shoop and Wallace to validate the selection and start the process to get the student to the United States.

After the interview it was determined that I would join the National Military Academy Implementation Team in what was to be a monumental task of establishing the first National Military Academy of Afghanistan (NMAA).

One of our primary tasks to accomplish was a briefing for Major General Weston. Approximately 99.99% of the presentation was put together by Shoop and Wallace. I think I said, "That looks good," once or twice during the work-up. However, as hard as they worked on the presentation, I don't think any of us were prepared for the comments that came from Major General Weston.

As we prepared our "Death by Power Point" presentation, we were patting ourselves on the back as to how good this would look. Colonel Shoop was the primary presenter and right in the middle of an outstanding display of knowledge and future successes, Major General Weston said, "You know you don't have any money for this mission."

I almost choked on those words. What was he talking about? No money! How did he expect us to accomplish our mission without proper funding?

That was only one of the issues I had coming to consider. Initially, we had a sixty-five million dollar budget to work with, but the reason it was cut to zero was because of the higher priority of establishing a secure environment for the upcoming election scheduled for October, 2004. The elections were a high profile issue, and it was imperative that they be conducted safely and efficiently. While I didn't agree that our funding should be cut so radically, I could not fault Major General Weston in his decision to make such a move. He was looking at a much bigger picture than me.

The other little surprise I had was the initial eight member full-time staff was cut to zero also. Why? Because personnel were needed in other areas of OMC-A, and the education issue, again, was not a high priority. As Major General Weston stated, "The academy is a nice-to-do thing." In other words, if we can get it done with minimal cost and personnel, then we will do it. I don't believe he initially thought it would come to pass. So we had a mission possible with two exceptions: No money and no permanent staff.

What I also found interesting was the reaction of Colonel Shoop during his presentation and finding out all the good news. He never missed a beat. He just plowed through his presentation like we had all the money in the world and the academy would become a reality.

After the briefing, I asked Colonel Shoop what he thought of Major General Weston's comments and he said the academy would be completed eventually and funding will happen. That didn't help my attitude toward this mission though. I thought I had been farmed off to a non-existent mission and after a year would come home with nothing accomplished.

Meanwhile, we had a lot of work to do and not a lot of time to complete the tasks at hand. It was time to develop some type of plan of action. I was still trying to figure out what my role was going to be in this mission.

PLANNING TO PLAN

B efore I can get to the issues I was involved with, I must first provide some background or historical reference as to what had been happening with this project. To say I began this project from scratch would not be factual.

Two West Point faculty, Colonel George Forsythe, Vice Dean of Education, and Lieutenant Colonel Casey Neff, Special Assistant to the Commandant for Systems and Planning were instrumental in getting the project in the planning stages. They conducted the research basically on site in Afghanistan and recommended the building of a military academy that would be modeled after the United States Military Academy at West Point, New York. Below is an excerpt from the introduction of their exhaustive work to establish a foundation.

"In August of 2003, Major General Karl Eikenberry, Office of Military Command—Afghanistan (OMC-A) Chief had requested support from LTG William Lennox, Superintendent, United States Military Academy, to establish a military academy in Afghanistan as part of the International Coalition's efforts to build the Afghan National Army (ANA) in accordance with the Bonn Agreement."

The Bonn Agreement was established in Bonn, Germany, to promote national reconciliation, lasting peace, stability, and respect for human rights in the country of Afghanistan. Afghanistan, in conjunction with the United Nations, established a sequence of events to aid in the establishment of a government that would be decided by a democratic vote which would include women for the first time in its history.

Over eight million people voted in the election, which constituted approximately seventy percent of the population of Afghanistan. Also, forty percent of the vote was from women. With the threats issued around the country, that is quite a turnout to show a force for change.

A concern for the future of Afghanistan revolved around education. During the Taliban era, women were no longer allowed to attend school, so their educational opportunities were non-existent.

Most of the brightest young men that graduated from high school (top one percent) went to medical school at Kabul University.

Many of the higher ranking officers had been educated in Russia for their advanced degrees, but now that was no longer an option. The noncommissioned officers were basically non-educated personnel, and there was a problem with soldiers breaking ranks and leaving the military to go back to their homes or to join other organizations that would promise them a better lifestyle.

To aid in the education of young officers, the Defense Ministry, along with Britain, Turkey, and the United States, conducted the study of what would be a better fit for the future of the Afghanistan National Army (ANA).

There were several players in this team, and a few should be mentioned because of the role they played in helping or hindering the accomplishment of our tasks and ultimately the mission of opening an academy for Afghanistan.

Colonel Forsythe and Lieutenant Colonel Neff represented the United States Military Academy at West Point. I do not know who represented the British, but Colonel Senor Tekbas represented Turkey. The Afghan Working Group Director was Major General Mohammad Juma Naser. His involvement later in the program became non-existent, as he was involved with other projects and objectives.

Colonel Tekbas was the Turkish Defense Attaché. This man was a piece of work and even though I considered him a friend, he would be a problem throughout the mission. His boasting of his accomplishments made me think that his promotions came from things he said he was going to do, not from things that he actually did. Major General Abdull Razak was the Military Academy Commander, and I thought he would be the new superintendent for the NMAA.

Brigadier General Mohammad Amin Wardak of the Military Academy Program of Instruction and Curriculum, Chief for Education, was a joy to work with and is one of the people I most respected in the Ministry of Defense.

Colonel Hamdullah, Military Academy Educational Deputy, later became the Dean of the NMAA. His son applied, competed, and was accepted to West Point as the first Afghan student to attend the United States Military Academy in West Point, New York.

I was fortunate that the stability of the officers I worked with at MoD was good. Our own forces, however, were another matter. When I arrived there had been a significant number of rotations in and out of the country.

Initially, Major General Karl Eikenberry was the Chief of the Office of Military Cooperation–Afghanistan. The initial development of the academy was actually his brain child. A couple of months later, Colonel Forsythe and Lieutenant Colonel Neff got involved and the players started to change. MG Eikenberry had redeployed back to the states.

The Military Academy Study Team (MAST) met with Brigadier General Prasek, the newly appointed OMC-A Chief, concerning the Academy status and future. Yes, Major General Eikenberry was gone and Brigadier General Prasek was his replacement. This was only the beginning of the changes. Brigadier General Prasek issued the following mission: *"Develop an organizational and operational concept for a National Military Academy of Afghanistan."*

There you have it. The seed was planted for Colonel Forsythe and Lieutenant Colonel Neff to start the planning process. It had to be affordable now and in the future. Initially, they wanted to look at a two year program and to expand into a four year program. There was the "Royal Military Academy at Sandhurst" model from Britain that was discussed, but the final decision was that the "West Point" model was what the Afghans wanted.

Sandhurst is not a university. While it is not a requirement, well over three-fourths of the candidates there are already university graduates. It provided initial training for British Officers.

West Point provides not only the military training, but additional educational work that would allow the students there to also receive a college degree in a variety of course offerings.

To even consider such a mission, there would need to be what seemed like hundreds of planning meetings. Everyone had an idea of how to make this happen, and there was a lot of posturing going on with personnel in the Ministry of Defense (MoD), as well as with Colonel Tekbas from Turkey. He was quick to tell everyone of the academy he built in the Country of Georgia, but after my experience with him on this mission, I will always wonder just what his role actually was in the previous academy.

A site needed to be located and numerous places were considered and evaluated. Kabul Military Training Center (KMTC), Pol-e-Charkhi, Qargha, some land east of Kabul University, Kabul Military High School, and the old Air Force University near the Kabul International Airport were some of the sites considered.

Another issue was related to the Ministry of Higher Education coordination, which involved Dr. Mohammad Sharif Fawzi, the Afghan Minister of Education. Through him, we had to work through problems and solutions that related to degrees, faculty, and administration.

I always enjoyed meeting with Dr. Fawzi at MoD. He was very hospitable and excited to have us over to discuss the future of education in Afghanistan. Since this was his area of expertise, I relied heavily on his suggestions and we developed a strong and professional relationship while planning and implementing the task for the academy. I will never forget the hug he gave me the day the academy opened. We were both smiling excitedly as we approached each other. I think it caught some of the soldiers both from Afghanistan and the United States off guard when we threw our arms around each other in a celebration of excitement as the first cadets were being in-processed to the National Military Academy of Afghanistan.

THE CROWN JEWEL CONCEPT IS BORN

As part of the education and degree requirements, there had to be many discussions as to the context and specific requirements that were needed for developing Afghan Officers.

Because the Afghan National Army was being rebuilt from the ground up, we felt we had the perfect opportunity to establish a leadership program for future officers that would go far beyond the National Military Academy of Afghanistan (NMAA). Already in the system was an officer's advanced course, and the French were conducting a Command and General Staff Course for senior grade officers.

Because of the major changes in the country, the NMAA was the long range target for success. I told everyone that would listen, from MoD to OMC-A, that the NMAA would be the Crown Jewel for Afghanistan, and I still believe that today!

In the planning stages, Colonel Forsythe and Lieutenant Colonel Neff had to take into consideration the Islamic role in the country. Also, diversity was an absolute must if we were to have representation of the many ethnic groups from around the country. This was going to be a tough assignment. These ethnic groups have been involved in conflict for many years, and you just don't get over the past overnight!

To address Brigadier General Prasek's guidance, Colonel Forsythe and Lieutenant Colonel Neff established a strategic concept for the military academy. This concept included a purpose, mission, graduate goals, and a concept of cadet development. It should be kept in mind that much of this information was adopted from West Point, but the Afghan leaders embraced this concept because of the professional work done and provided by Forsythe and Neff. They are excellent salesmen.

The following statement identifies the Purpose and Mission Statement of the NMAA as proposed by the committee from the USMA and MoD:

> *Purpose of the National Military Academy of Afghanistan*
> *To provide the Afghan National Army with professional*
> *officers who support and defend the Constitution of the*
> *Islamic State of Afghanistan and are faithful to its*
> *national principles, laws and regulations.*
> *Mission of the National Military Academy of Afghanistan*
> *To educate, train, and inspire the Cadet Brigade so that*
> *each graduate is a competent, courageous, and honorable*
> *officer in the Afghan National Army committed to continuous*
> *professional development and a lifetime of military and civilian*
> *service to the nation.*

With the above mission and purpose statements, Forsythe and Neff took a systematic approach to developing a curriculum design. This was done through a combination of a knowledge-base they had of curriculum development at West Point and an "upfront" needs assessment in an extremely compressed amount of time.

Their work involved a significant amount of open discussion and brainstorming; the Afghans were not used to operating in such an environment. Afghans basically operated from the top down without any discussion. (I will have to admit that such a format, at times, came in handy when we had to move forward toward our objective.)

Forsythe and Neff had to do their analysis, propose a tentative solution, write it up, translate into Dari for the Afghans, then meet with them for discussion. The individuals whom were really pushed to the limit were the Afghan translators, Dr. Sardar and Mr. Masoom. Throughout the mission they were constantly put in a 'crash' mode to finish the job and have it ready for the Afghans to read, think about and provide feedback that would help them declare ownership in the academy.

I contacted Colonel Forsythe for his thoughts concerning his initial experience with the planning of the academy. Below are the comments he shared:

> The curriculum developed was actually a creative hybrid of several solutions. Certainly a common academic core curriculum; however our draw near to military training and academic specialty education (a major) is not like West Point's, in that we tied the academic specialty to the military specialty. We also tried to be very sensitive to the specific course needs, although again, the Afghan participation came once we had proposed something, not in the conceptualization stages.
>
> I believe we saw our mission as two-fold: Develop a feasible plan, but more importantly, establish a trusting working relationship with the Afghans that would sustain their involvement in and commitment to the Military Academy. I think we succeeded. One senior Afghan general told me we were the first foreigners who actually listened to them. I considered that high praise.

This was the foundation we used and continued to emphasize as we tried to sell the "Crown Jewel" concept to MoD. It was important to establish effective communications if we were going to be successful. A trust between the players was extremely important.

That trust was validated one day when a particularly sensitive issue arose, and in visiting with Brigadier General Amen, I made the comment, "General, you are just going to have to trust me on this." His reply was, "I trust you more than one hundred percent." At that moment I realized we were going to make great strides in the completion of our mission.

I also found out the Afghans will argue until they are red in the face over issues, but once it is signed in a written document, it becomes law and that particular issue came back to haunt me on more than one occasion. As I mentioned earlier, the country was changing so rapidly that long-range plans were out of the question. The initial plan for the academy had us building very nice facilities. It was put in writing, but we were unable to use the money for that purpose because the cost of providing the election security was seen as a higher priority. I was reminded on numerous occasions that the United States promised facilities to be built at sites that had been agreed on in writing. We did not have the money or the time to build it from the ground up.

Forsythe and Neff presented two options to MoD. One was a two-year curriculum and the other a four-year curriculum. There was concern to get educated officers to the Afghan National Army (ANA) as soon as possible, as well as to define an obtainable goal that could be funded through the efforts of the coalition forces and MoD. There was also an initial concern of identifying qualified professors to teach the students. All concerns were justified, but we also wanted to consider the future of the educational state of the country.

Because of the twenty-five plus years of war, higher education was in trouble to say the least. The four-year curriculum would incorporate the use of technology, decision making, military strategies, honor, code of conduct, and educational issues that would make the graduate a significantly productive member of his country. We were going after the best and brightest kids that represented ethnic balance within the country so our investment would have a long-term effect beyond military service.

LET'S BUILD IT HERE. NO HERE. NO RIGHT HERE!

The site was a significant issue for discussion and debate. The option recommended by the Military Academy Study Team (MAST) was to locate the academy on a tract of land south of Qargha near the village of Spin Kalay. While recommended, it was not the site that was chosen because of funding issues I mentioned earlier.

While the site was a significant piece of the puzzle, so was the selection of the faculty. This country had been at war for the past twenty-five years, so the educational expertise was somewhat lacking. Ideally, we wanted people with graduate degrees but had to settle on bachelor degrees for the most part. For the faculty, having a current knowledge-base in the field they taught was also important. We found out later, during the interviews, that what is current in Afghanistan may not be current in our country.

An issue dealing with the staffing of faculty related to the hiring of military and/or civilian personnel. It was recommended by the MAST that, because of the educational qualifications of faculty at Kabul University as well as other educational institutions, a combination of military and civilian personnel be hired.

We also had to deal with the issues of salaries for military and civilian personnel. In Afghanistan, a public school teacher makes the equivalent of forty U.S. dollars per month. If he/she is lucky, a tent will also be provided in outlying areas. It was not unusual to see kids in open areas or bombed out buildings holding classes. It certainly made me appreciate what I have in the United States classrooms.

Medical doctors make approximately seventy dollars per month, so it was an extremely poor country based on these two examples. It was basically the norm that families, including mothers, fathers, in-laws, grandparents, children, etc. all lived together and worked to pool their income so they could survive.

One of the final objectives identified by Colonel Forsythe and Lieutenant Colonel Neff was that of an Implementation Plan followed by an Implementation Tasking document. Part of the implementation plan would give us the guidance to begin building this program to its ultimate success. The following objectives had to be reached before the February 2005 opening date of the academy: Faculty, staff, and cadets had to be selected; academy facilities had to be constructed; supplies and equipment had to be obtained; regulations, instructional materials, lesson plans, policies, and standard operating procedures needed to be written and published; and operations and maintenance funding to establish and sustain the academy had to be planned, programmed, budgeted, and available. That was not all, but it was certainly enough to get us started.

In that same Implementation Plan paragraph was a statement that read: "Assuming resource availability, the expectation is that the NMAA will open in the spring of 2005." Each morning as we identified our goals and objectives for the day I would always close with the comment, "Let's GIT 'R Done." We would then depart for our work day. It was imperative that we experienced success every day we went outside the wire. That was the only way we could monitor our success. We were going to have an academy someway, somehow, by the spring of 2005.

It had been recommended that the Implementation Support Team (IST) be headed by a Colonel or Lieutenant Colonel on a one year assignment and staffed by eight civilian contractors. The mission of the IST would be to advise the ANA Implementation Team and coordinate coalition support for the implementation of the concept plan. According to the MAST report, the IST should include individuals with the following expertise:

Team Chief: Colonel or Lieutenant Colonel on a one-year assignment, preferably with recent USMA experience.

Academy Specialist: with expertise in Curriculum, Assessment Academic

Planning and Admissions (will also coordinate with the Ministry of Higher Education)

Military and Physical Training Specialist

Engineer Project Manager

Supply and Services Specialist

Contracting Specialist

Personnel/Force Development Specialist

Telecom/Information Technology Specialist

The IST should draw on OMC-A staff for expertise in the following areas: medical, dental, legal, security, and force protection, recruiting, and construction.

This was a great team.

I could understand the one year assignment, because of the magnitude of the mission, but I thought the one year tour of the Colonel or lieutenant Colonel would also include a one year tour of the other personnel. This was not the case and made my mission extremely frustrating, interesting, busy, fun, and/or scary. Pick any words you want or make up your own. I went through all the emotions one can imagine during my year there.

Next, the Implementation Task List was submitted. This is what needed to be completed to make the mission successful. Again, Colonel Forsythe and Lieutenant Colonel Neff should be commended for the detailed work that needed to be done. While it was overwhelming, at times, to accomplish, the completion of these tasks was the force that drove this mission ahead and to its ultimate successful completion. The Implementation Task List is provided for you to get an idea of what lay ahead for the MAIST.

Implementation Tasks

Mission: Establish the National Military Academy of Afghanistan and begin operations with the first class of cadet in February 2005.

Task List	Action Agency	Status	Suspense
1. NMAA manned with qualified faculty, support staff, and cadets			
1.A. <u>Staff the NMAA with qualified staff and faculty prepared to begin operations in February 2005</u>			
1.A.(1) Develop complete TDA—positions, grades, and pay scales			
1.A.(2) Recruit, Select, and Hire faculty			
1.A.(3) Train faculty			
1.A.(4) Select support staff			
1.A.(5) Train support staff			
1.B. <u>Staff the Cadet Brigade with a class of 350 best- qualified cadets representing the ethnic diversity of the country</u>			

	Task List	Action Agency	Status	Suspense
1.B.(1)	Select first class of cadets			
1.B.(2)	Prepare admissions policies and procedures			
1.B.(3)	Organize, Equip, Train, and Staff the Academy Admission Office			
1.B.(4)	Prepare training materials for NAVC recruiters			
1.B.(5)	Train NAVC Recruiters			
1.B.(6)	Identify qualified cadet candidates			
1.B.(7)	Evaluate files based on admissions criteria			
1.B.(8)	Select and place in rank-order 500 best qualified, consistent with ethnicity goals			
1.B.(9)	Offer admissions until class of 350 is filled			

Task List	Action Agency	Status	Suspense
2. NMAA constructed and ready to begin operations in February 2005			
2.A. <u>Obtain and Prepare the Site for the NMAA</u>			
2.A.(1) Select site for NMAA			
2.A.(2) Obtain funds to purchase site (if necessary)			
2.A.(3) Conduct title search			
2.A.(4) Purchase site (if necessary)			
2.A.(5) Prepare site for construction			
2.B. <u>Complete Cadet Support Facilities</u>: *barracks, mess hall, medical clinic, force protection, mosque*			
2.B.(1) Identify cadet support facilities requirements			

Task List	Action Agency	Status	Suspense
2.B.(2) Obtain funds to design cadet support facilities			
2.B.(2)(a)Obtain non-US funds for construction of mosque			
2.B.(3) Complete design cadet support facilities			
2.B.(4) Start construction of cadet support facilities			
2.B.(5) Complete construction of cadet support facilities			
2.C. Complete Essential Infrastructure: water, sewage, power (electricity), transportation (roads, parking lots), telecom, information technology			
2.C.(1) Identify essential infrastructure requirements			

Task List	Action Agency	Status	Suspense
2.C.(2) Obtain funds to design essential infrastructure			
2.C.(3) Complete design of essential infrastructure			
2.C.(4) Start construction and installation of essential infrastructure			
2.C.(5) Complete construction and installation of essential infrastructure			
2.D. Complete Essential Stationing Facilities: *headquarters, administration, classrooms, athletic facilities, training facilities, ranges, MWR, supply, storage, maintenance*			
2.D.(1) Identify essential stationing facilities requirements			

Task List	Action Agency	Status	Suspense
2.D.(2) Obtain funds to design essential stationing facilities			
2.D.(3) Complete design of essential sta-tioning facilities			
2.D.(4) Start construction of essential sta-tioning facilities			
2.D.(5) Complete construction of essential station-ing facilities			
3. Required equipment installed and on hand to begin operations in February 2005			
3.A. Obtain and Install Essential Cadet Support Equipment: *barracks furniture, mess hall furniture and equipment, medi-cal clinic furniture and equipment , mosque furnishing*			

Task List	Action Agency	Status	Suspense
3.A.(1) Identify essential cadet support equipment requirements			
3.A.(2) Obtain funds for cadet support equipment			
3.A.(2)(a) Obtain non-US funds for mosque equipment			
3.A.(3) Purchase cadet support equipment			
3.A.(4) Receive cadet support equipment			
3.A.(5) Install or store cadet support equipment			

Task List	Action Agency	Status	Suspense
3.B. <u>Obtain and Install Essential Cadet Instructional Equipment</u>: *classroom furniture; library furniture; classroom and lab equipment; library materials, books, & equipment; computers; military equipment; athletic & physical training equipment; school supplies; textbooks; cadet uniforms and clothing*			
3.B.(1) Identify essential cadet instructional equipment requirements			
3.B.(2) Obtain funds for cadet instructional equipment			
3.B.(3) Purchase cadet instructional equipment			
3.B.(4) Receive cadet instructional equipment			

Task List	Action Agency	Status	Suspense
3.B.(5) Install or Store cadet instructional equipment			
3.C. Obtain and Install Essential Stationing Equipment: *office furniture; office supplies; network equipment, mess hall equipment, medical clinic equipment*			
3.C.(1) Identify essential stationing equipment requirements			
3.C.(2) Obtain funds for stationing equipment			
3.C.(3) Purchase stationing equipment			
3.C.(4) Receive stationing equipment			
3.C.(5) Install or store stationing equipment			

Task List	Action Agency	Status	Suspense
4. Essential Regulations, Plans, Policies, and Procedures are prepared and published			
4.A. <u>Prepare and Publish Academy Regulations, Plans, Policies and Procedures</u>: *command relationships (where NMAA fit into ANA structure); NMAA Organization and Functions; personnel (military and civilian): recruitment, selection, hiring, management and career development, compensation, promotion, records management; standards: admission, retention, graduation, and commissioning of cadet; active duty service obligation of cadets; assignment of graduates; information management; resource management (PPBS)*			

Task List	Action Agency	Status	Suspense
4.A.(1) Write academy regulations, plans, policies, and procedures			
4.A.(2) Staff academy regulations, plans, policies, and procedures with relevant MoD, GS, Education and Training Command, and OMC-A ANA PDT agencies.			
4.A.(3) Print academy regulations, plans, policies, and procedures			
4.A.(4) Distribute academy regulations, plans, policies, and procedures			

Task List	Action Agency	Status	Suspense
4.B. <u>Prepare and Publish Academic Regulations, Plans. Policies, and Procedures</u>: *curriculum; catalog; course syllabi; instructional materials; classroom procedures; examination and grading procedures; academic awards; procedures for scheduling classrooms and assigning cadets to courses; faculty manual (employment, compensation, performance expectations, academic freedom, faculty code of ethics, research expectations); faculty credentials and promotions; computer use policies*			
4.B.(1) Write academic regulations, plans, policies, and procedures			

Task List	Action Agency	Status	Suspense
4.B.(2) Staff academic regulations, plans, policies, and procedures with relevant MoD, GS, Education and Training Command, and OMC-A ANA PDT agencies.			
4.B.(3) Print academic regulations, plans, policies, and procedures			
4.B.(4) Distribute academic regulations, plans, policies, and procedures			

Task List	Action Agency	Status	Suspense
4.C. <u>Prepare and Publish Cadet Brigade Regulations, Plans, Policies and Procedures</u>: *Military Program; Physical Program; Organization and Functions; Regulations and Discipline for the Cadet Brigade; Honor code and System; Leadership Development and Evaluation system; cadet leave and pass; cadet uniforms*			
4.C.(1) Write Cadet Brigade regulations, plans, policies, and procedures			
4.C.(2) Staff Cadet Brigade regulations, plans, policies, and procedures with relevant MoD, GS, Education and Training Command, and OMC-A ANA PDT agencies.			
4.C.(3) Print Cadet Brigade regulations, plans, policies, and procedures			

Task List	Action Agency	Status	Suspense
4.C.(4) Distribute Cadet Brigade regulations, plans, policies, and procedures			
4.D. Prepare and Publish Support Battalion Regulations, Plans, Policies, and Procedures: *transportation; supply and services; medical and dental; security and force protection; operations*			
4.D.(1) Write support battalion regulations, plans, policies, and procedures			
4.D.(2) Staff support battalion regulations, plans, policies, and procedures with relevant MoD, GS, Education and Training Command, and OMC-A ANA PDT agencies.			

Task List	Action Agency	Status	Suspense
4.D.(3) Print support battalion regulations, plans, policies, and procedures			
4.D.(4) Distribute support battalion regulations, plans, policies, and procedures			
5. Operation and maintenance funds are identified, budgeted, and on-hand to sustain NMAA operations			
5.A. Identify O&M requirements			
5.B. Submit O&M budget			
5.C. Obtain O&M funds			

Colonel Forsythe and Lieutenant Colonel Neff were followed by Lieutenant Colonel Donna Brazil and Major William Caruso, both from West Point. Brazil and Caruso were scheduled to be there for six weeks with the follow-on mission to further develop the operational and organizational concept plan for the NMAA. According to Lieutenant Colonel Brazil's report, their mission was to serve as a bridge between the Military Academy Study team and the work it conducted in October-November 2003 and the Military Academy Implementation Team that was to begin operation in June 2004 (where I came in), and see the Academy through its opening in February 2005. Her team, which included the previous Afghan and Turkish group, was charged with writing, discussing, and agreeing (possibly the hardest) on policies to assist the organizational structure, recruiting, selection, and other supporting tasks. They also worked the issues related to budgeting, coordination, and execution.

Many of the tasks that we were to address later were initially addressed by Lieutenant Colonel Brazil and Major Caruso. I mentioned earlier that at times the written word from the work done by the previous teams came back to haunt me when we had to adjust our mission in order for it to be completed and the opening to be on time. However, I will also say these written documents put together by the teams came in very handy when there was, at times, a bit of forgetfulness with the Afghan leadership.

On Brazil and Caruso's watch came the problem of the actual location of the academy. Initially, it was to be at Qargha, in the southern part of Kabul, but because of funding constraints, that was no longer an option. That issue was a thorn throughout my tenure there. However, we were able to reflect on the team's report that as early as January 2004, Qargha was off the table and other sites were being considered, including the Air Academy and Kabul Military High School.

Lieutenant Colonel Brazil and Major Caruso's work was extremely well thought out and a fantastic foundation from which we were able to work during the building of the initial phases of the academy. Throughout this book you will find me reflecting on the work of these two outstanding officers and their contribution to the success of the National Military Academy of Afghanistan.

LTC Brazil's final report was submitted on February 8, 2004, which indicates there was approximately a three month time frame where not much was going on. Progressive action did not actually take place until Colonel Shoop and Lieutenant Colonel Wallace arrived on the scene with me tagging along for the ride of my life.

POLICY/DOCTRINE/ CURRICULUM/PERSONNEL DEVELOPMENT

I hate meetings; boy, was I ever in the wrong environment at this time in my life. For us to build a university of the magnitude that was expected, we were going to be required to meet daily in order to identify objectives and stay on task to complete our mission.

It would be absolutely essential that our plans be put in writing and signed off by both the U.S. forces and the Afghans. We had to have a policy/doctrine written almost immediately. This would be the foundation for success, so it was imperative that we would be in agreement with our Afghan counterparts. The curriculum and personnel development could come later.

I quickly came to the conclusion that the Afghans loved meetings and there was a particular way meetings always seemed to start. I also quickly realized that was basically a 'non-negotiable' custom and, therefore, I did not interfere with how meetings were held. About a month into my mission I began to really appreciate this format.

While many of the Afghans I met with were soldiers, warriors, and God knows what else, they were truly hospitable. I don't think I had ever met a more gracious group of people. While their country was poor and they were poor, their generosity came straight from the heart and was priceless. I learned this was not just the situation with the officials I met, but is fairly standard across the country. It was widely known and accepted that Afghans would show more hospitality than their economic limits would allow, whether for a close friend, family member or perfect stranger. That was a values lesson I learned early on in my mission. I pray to God that I can be as gracious a host as the friends I met in Afghanistan.

Afghan meetings started in this sequence. There were introductions and welcomes, followed by the right hand laid across the chest as a greeting, and then handshakes. If the individuals knew each other more closely, there would be an occasional hug. Our host would invite us to sit for hot tea, called chai, and a series of nuts and fruits. To show our western influence in the country, chai would occasionally be replaced by Pepsi drinks. We would visit with our host for twenty to thirty minutes before any business was conducted. During that time, we were expected to have three cups of tea. The three cups reflects your respect for your host. After some informal visiting and the three cups of tea, we would finally get down to business. For a society like ours, the time out for three cups of tea might drive some people crazy. This custom should be looked at more seriously though. We have all been told at one time or another, "Slow down and smell the roses." In this particular case, we would drink instead of smell.

There were also a few terms that were used at these meetings that would, at times, catch me off guard. Eventually, I got used to their banter and forged ahead just like I knew what they were talking about. However, at one particular meeting, I was told by a member of the Minister of Defense, "First we will have chai then we will fight."

Well, this is very interesting. I had heard the Afghans would fight at the drop of a hat if they felt threatened about something they truly believed. Dr. Sardar, my translator, could tell immediately that I was alarmed by the gentleman's comment, so he translated the statement as, "First we will have chai then we will meet, visit, discuss, debate, and eventually come to an agreement." I felt much better after that. Initially, I thought one of us was going to get beat up severely, and the odds were not going to be in my favor.

The leaders I met with were always looking for solutions. They would brainstorm many options and always would be in agreement that whatever was decided could be done and done well. The only problem was to have it approved at the next level. If there was a road block in the approval and implementation process, then the chain of command was it. Initiative in making a decision without approval from higher headquarters was almost non-existent.

I found out that many decisions basically funneled from the top down. Because decisions came from the top of the leadership chain, it often did not matter what was discussed below. I found out quickly that I worked many days at the wrong end of the power curve.

I spent more and more time at the Ministry of Defense (MoD) offices working with Minister of Defense Abdul Rahim Wardak, as well as the other ministers. It was absolutely essential that I gained the trust of the personnel in the Ministry of Defense. Once that was established, the objectives started to come together for the establishment of the academy.

When an agreement of a particular objective was finally established, it was important that we put it in writing. That may sound reasonable, but it was not as easy as one might think. It first had to be translated and written in Dari, the primary native language in Afghanistan. After Dr. Sardar or Mr. Masoom translated and printed the agreement in Dari, the interpretation by MoD personnel might see the document as something with which they could not agree. It was not unusual for the Afghans to come back to me and say the previous team put together a document in writing that said a particular issue could and would happen. It did not match what we had discussed and had just translated. This was never brought to my attention before all the work was done.

Of course, I did not have the documents they were talking about with me, and more times than not, they could not produce them. It became apparent that we both had drawn a line in the dirt and were beginning to challenge any and everything that had happened before I arrived.

It should be noted that we were still in the planning phase. We had no staff, faculty, facilities, money, nor students. All we actually had were words.

Colonel Shoop was as patient an individual as I had ever seen, but it was obvious that his patience was being stretched to the limit. Lieutenant Colonel Wallace spent many hours typing up the notes he had taken. This is the translation and problem we seemed to be having. After a couple of weeks it began to wear on both Lieutenant Colonel Wallace and Colonel Shoop. I could tell these guys needed a break or at least a distraction to get them off the problems we were having.

At this particular time, I wasn't as much help as I probably should have been, but I did not worry too much about it. I thought these two gentlemen would be with me for the duration of one year. I was not aware that I would eventually be handed the reins and saddle and told to ride this horse.

These two had not spent much time in the Midwest, so I decided I would introduce them to a game we play in Oklahoma and Texas and to the culture I came from.

I sat them down one evening and taught them how to play a domino game called "Forty-two," which required four participants to be involved. (If you only had three people, then the game was called "Moon"). We needed a fourth person to make this happen and so we drug in Major Eric Arnoldus, who had also been assigned to join this team on a temporary basis.

I informed them that to play this game correctly, they had to be in the mindset of a good old southern boy, so I wanted to introduce a video that would set the mood. I indicated that, while I didn't know the people on the video personally, I did know people that had this type of background and I could see myself in many of their stories. The men in that video just took it to a new level. I introduced it with the following statement, "Gentlemen this is where I come from. This is what I am about." With that I began the "Blue Collar Comedy Tour" with Larry the Cable Guy, Bill Engvall, Jeff Foxworthy, and Ron White.

It was so well received by Colonel Shoop and Lieutenant Colonel Wallace that I decided to make it an introduction to all future West Point personnel that came to Afghanistan. I probably was responsible for a significant number of sales in dominos and "The Blue Collar Comedy Tour" based on how I introduced it. "Git 'R Done," "I don't think so, scooter," "Here's your sign," and "You might be a redneck," became a staple of our conversations during our mission. It was probably one of the more significant breaks from an extremely stressful situation, because it would always bring a smile or a laugh, depending on the environment and situation.

After the video was shown, I would then begin the rules for "Forty-two." You must understand, I had to have them in the right mindset before we could begin anything as strategic as dominoes. It was important to be able to analyze the dominoes and determine who has played, what was played, and what needed to be played next. Also, alcohol was not allowed on our base, or anywhere for that matter, and it made the total understanding of the game that much more difficult, or so I thought.

I must have been one heck of a teacher. After just a few rounds, these guys were kicking my butt. At first I thought it must have been my ability to teach the objectives of the game, but later realized with one being head of the electrical engineering department, and the other an attorney at West Point, and Major Arnoldus being a CPA, I didn't stand a chance. These guys could analyze the spots off the dominoes. It wasn't that I was a great teacher; they were just great students.

That pattern continued throughout my tour of Afghanistan with the West Point personnel. Of course, these were the deans and department heads that were coming over, and the brain trust was something I was not ready for. They did not get to the positions they were in without a significant amount of intelligence. Anything mathematical was very easy for them to master.

Regardless of who won or lost, the break from the routine of meetings and slow progress that was being made was welcomed by everyone. We still had to attend the meetings the following day and try as hard as we could to get the Afghan leaders to commit to a decision and move forward with the building of the academy.

OKLAHOMA PROVERBS

As mentioned earlier, many of our participants were somewhat reluctant to make a decision and would wait for higher-ups to give the approval. It was quite frustrating to get people, "Off the nickel" so to speak, and move forward. When things would get a bit tense, we would be told of an Afghan proverb.

When an Afghan says, "In our country, we have an Afghan Proverb . . ." people will stop what they are doing and listen. I am reminded of the commercial, "When E.F. Hutton speaks, people listen."

Unfortunately, for this Oklahoma boy, most of the proverbs did not make much sense. That is not a statement against the Afghans, just my cultural upbringing. On more than one occasion, I would get this deer in the headlights look. I can't speak for Colonel Shoop and Lieutenant Colonel Wallace. They probably understood the proverbs. After all, they certainly understood "Forty-two." I learned to just nod my head and smile. Later, I would ask Dr. Sardar what the proverb meant.

After a while I began to have a better understanding as to what they were saying in the proverbs. However, I can't help but think they changed the proverbs around a bit so I could understand them better.

For example, I remember one so-called proverb that was quoted to a Turkish official that made a great point. It was well into my tour, and Colonel Shoop and Lieutenant Colonel Wallace had already returned to West Point. It is one that I will always remember, and it is something we should all consider if we want to get a message across to someone without being out of line too much.

During a particular testy time, well into our mission, one Turkish official was beginning to irritate Major General Sharif, our future Superintendent of the National Military Academy of Afghanistan. General Sharif folded his arms, leaned back in his chair, and referenced an Afghan proverb that says, "Two men cannot ride the same donkey." The Turkish official said he did not understand why the General would say that and he did not know what it meant. Sharif replied, "My friend, it is simple, get off my ass!" He looked at me, nodded his head, and laughed. Good job, General! I don't know if that was actually an Afghan proverb, but the timing was fantastic and put the Turkish official in his place.

There were times where I even used proverbs. They were not Afghan Proverbs but Oklahoma Proverbs. Many people, including Oklahomans, did not even know we had proverbs beyond "Git 'R Done," or something else from the Blue Collar Comedy Tour. Actually, I don't think we do, but I had to grasp at anything I could to help with the communications issues and understandings.

For example, during the initial phases of the development of the academy I had realized early on that we were not moving at the pace that would be necessary for the successful completion of our mission. In fact, we were at a complete standstill. During one particular meeting where the discussions and decision-making seemed to grind to a halt, I brought up an Oklahoma Proverb.

We were meeting with Major General Amin in his office and I desperately wanted us to move forward, so I made the following comment to General Amin: "Sir, in Oklahoma we have this proverb that might help with our situation." Colonel Shoop and Lieutenant Colonel Wallace looked at each other then at me with a sort of strange look, like I had just lost my mind. Everyone in the room got quiet, but for different reasons: the Afghans because they wanted to hear this proverb and how it would guide them, and Shoop and Wallace because they had just watched the Blue Collar Comedy Tour and wondered just what kind of nonsense I was going to say.

I indicated that in Oklahoma we say, "One must continue to push the snowball down the hill or else it will melt." At the same time, I put my hands together, palms down, and gave a rolling motion like I was pushing the snowball down the hill.

The look I got from Shoop and Wallace was definitely that of, "Wilhite has lost his mind and we are going to have to shoot him."

The Afghans reaction to my proverb was completely different. Their eyes lit up and they started doing the hand motion and saying, "Yes! Yes! We must continue to move forward or the snowball we have built will melt!" The snowball represented the progress we had made with the initial work of the academy.

That proverb was used many times during my stay while building the academy. It worked its way up through the Ministry of Defense chain of command, and we would refer to it in both positive and negative communications. It got to a point where the simple hand motion and a smile or frown would indicate whether we were on track or not.

Shoop and Wallace wanted to know where I heard of such a proverb, and I had to admit that I made it up on the spot and was just trying to get us to move forward. That wouldn't be the last time I came up with an Oklahoma Proverb.

At the time of the initial meetings, we had no superintendent for the academy, or anyone else for that matter from the academy. There were no positions approved or selected for the academy. The primary group for the meetings was composed of Brigadier General Amin, Assistant Minister of Education and Personnel, a

Major Taj from Turkey, who was taking Colonel Tekbas's place, Colonel Humdullah, who was from the old military air defense school, Colonel Shoop, Lieutenant Colonel Wallace, and myself.

Colonel Shoop conducted the meetings with Lieutenant Colonel Wallace providing input and seemed to be taking notes. I sat alongside them, fat, dumb, and happy, while at the same time still trying to figure why I was even here.

As daily meetings took place, I did not realize what Shoop and Wallace had in store for me. They continually talked of the MAIST (Military Academy Implementation Support Team) and the MAIT (Military Academy Implementation Team), but I thought they were talking about the same thing. The difference between the two was fairly simple.

The MAIST was the support group that was coming from West Point for thirty to forty-five days. The MAIT was the permanent party group that would be staying for the duration of the mission. Notice the word "Team" in each title. The Military Academy Implementation Support Team consisted of personnel who came before Shoop and Wallace. It also included Shoop and Wallace, as well as anyone that followed them.

The Military Academy Implementation Team consisted of me. Me! That's it! No other personnel. Go build a university! You have ten months! You have no full-time personnel! You have a support team that will be coming from West Point for thirty to forty-five days to support your mission. I did not realize I was being groomed for the most important, as well as the most challenging, mission of my military career.

Even at this time, I still thought my job was to be their comic relief. Other than the "Forty-two" game and the "Blue Collar Comedy Tour," I was pretty much out of material. There was one incident about Colonel Shoop and his flyswatter, but he will have to write his own version of the account.

As we conducted our meetings, we found ourselves driving all over Kabul. It's called going outside the wire. There were times, though, that going outside the wire could get a little tense.

For example, early in our tour we had to travel through Kabul to the military high school. It was our first major trip with Dr. Sardar, and he got turned around with his directions. Let's set the scene: First we have two Colonels and one lieutenant Colonel, each having an M-9 pistol. That is tense right there, senior officers with weapons. Next we have Dr. Sardar, our translator. He has no weapon, just his knowledge of how to get around town. We were to visit with the superintendent at the high school about some policies that had been written, as well as view the site as a possible location for the new academy.

In the middle of Kabul, we got in a traffic jam. We were in a sea of motorized vehicles, horse-drawn wagons, and people walking in the middle of the street. Basically, we were unable to move in any direction. We were a perfect target.

Dr. Sardar was not sure if we should turn right or left at a fork in the road up ahead, so he told us he is going to go check out the situation and immediately gets out of the SUV we were in and disappears in the crowd. Colonel Shoop and I look at each other and then turn to Lieutenant Colonel Wallace to see the color disappear from his face.

Where did Dr. Sardar go? What are we going to do if the crowd gets out of line? We decided to get our pistols ready, so we withdrew them from our holsters and prepared for the worst. As I reflect on the issue, the worst that might have happened would have been one of us shooting the other while we were trying to get our pistols out of the holsters. Basically, we didn't know whether to shoot or go blind.

We were prepared for the inevitable though, because Dr. Sardar was still nowhere in sight. As far as we knew, he had possibly set us up for ambush. That's how little we knew about Dr. Sardar.

All of a sudden, the mass of humanity parts like Moses's work with the Red Sea and there stands Dr. Sardar, motioning us to drive toward him. As we did, he walked ahead of us, directing vehicles, buggies, and people so that we could get through the multitudes and onward to Kabul Military High School. That was only one situation, of many, where Dr. Sardar solidified his commitment to the United States soldiers and our mission in Afghanistan.

I mentioned earlier that Lieutenant Colonel Wallace provided limited input and mainly took notes of the proceedings. Note taking was just a small contribution that he made. Lieutenant Colonel Wallace also observed the non-verbal communication that was taking place in the meetings. Because of his legal training, Lieutenant Colonel Wallace was very astute at people reading and interpreting what they were actually saying. After we would complete a meeting, Wallace and Shoop would evaluate what was actually said; at the same, time they received valuable feedback from Dr. Sardar. As I became more comfortable, I would also join in the conversation, and as their time started growing shorter, I became involved more and more in the process.

Every one of the MoD leaders were involved at one time or another in the policy and doctrine phase, as well as the Superintendent of the Kabul Military High School, the President of Kabul University, and the Minister of Higher Education. Education was a much needed commodity, and these individuals were eager to brainstorm possible ideas. These meetings were the building blocks for the establishment of the NMAA, and I was about to become its foreman!

ADDITIONAL DUTY ASSIGNMENT

I also had other responsibilities besides just building the academy. These responsibilities would surface with a short turn around time to complete. I was not the exception to this situation. Everyone at OMC-A was in a situation where they had to complete whatever mission was to take place. The environment was changing so rapidly that no one could predict the future more than a couple of weeks out. As a result, monitoring and adjusting was the standard, not the exception, and as stated earlier, Major General Weston was a master at making such adjustments.

A case in point was when I was asked to serve on a review board for selection of candidates of the Command and General Staff College that was being run by the French Army. OMC-A needed a representative to sit on that board. Since I was more of an observer of the academy planning stage rather than a participant, I agreed to participate. I had also taught the Command and General Staff College courses for many years, and was familiar with its operation and selection process.

Command and General Staff College, in the U.S., was required for promotion to Lieutenant Colonel and eventually Colonel. This particular Command and General Staff College designed by the French was to develop a better education and selection process for future senior leaders in the Afghan Army. Until that time, many selections for promotion were considered on war, fighting, and/or bravery.

I was introduced to Dr. Shahee, who was to be my translator. We became friends very quickly. He was a small man with a love for the U.S. intervention. He desperately wanted the U.S. to bring stability in his life and his country. Like many of our translators, his friends did not really know what he was doing for work. It had to be kept a secret, or he and his family could very easily be killed.

As Dr. Shahee and I sat at a table in the Command and General Staff College facility, I noticed a particular question/answer format begin to take place. It went as follows:

- The French Colonel would ask a question.

- It would be translated from French to Dari by his translator.

- While it was being translated to Dari, Dr. Shahee would translate the Dari to English for me.

- The candidate would give his response either in Dari or Pashtun and both translators would translate in French or English to either me or the French Colonel.

- If I had a question, the translation was reversed from English, to Dari, to French, etc.

This would go on for about four hours, then we would take a break for lunch. That afternoon we would start again for about four hours.

After the first thirty minutes of this exercise, I looked at Dr. Shahee and said, "I think my head is about to explode."

Dr. Shahee smiled and said in a soft voice, "Don't worry, sir, you will get used to it." Eventually I did.

One particular interview will always stick in my mind as being a bit frightening and funny at the same time. A candidate sat down for an interview and as I reviewed his records, I saw where he had absolutely no educational training whatsoever. However, he was a lieutenant Colonel in the Afghan Army. My first question to him was, "Without any educational training, how did you make lieutenant Colonel?"

The candidate screamed, "War!" which made me and the French Colonel jump.

"Please explain your association with the war." And he did.

His explanation would have made our most decorated American hero, Medal of Honor recipient Audie Murphy, nervous.

I turned to Dr. Shahee and said, "What is his position with his unit."

"He is an ex-ah-cutive officer."

"You mean he executes people? That's one tough unit!"

"No sir, he is in charge of the administrative details in the unit."

Okay, one of my many lessons was the emphasis is sometimes put on the wrong syllable and the meaning would get misinterpreted. At least by me!

After four full days of interviews, we had made our selections, and I was ready to get back to the planning stages of the academy. The selection process was a fantastic, but mentally tiring, short mission. I made many friends with the Afghan personnel, as well as the French officers and other personnel that were involved with the Command and General Staff College.

Another short mission we had to deal with was the selection of the first Afghan student that would be attending West Point. This was a historical moment in itself. The interviews were being held while I was at the Command and General Staff College interviews, and initially conducted by Colonel Shoop, Lieutenant Colonel Wallace, and Lieutenant Colonel Brazil.

They interviewed many students for this prestigious position and finally selected a young man named Shoiab Yosoufzai to be the first West Point Candidate.

Shoiab was the son of Colonel Hamdulla, the future Dean of Education at the National Military Academy of Afghanistan. While the selection process was difficult, the process of getting him to the U.S. was even more difficult.

Shoop, Wallace, and I went to the U.S. Embassy and visited with a representative named Derek Hodgson. We needed to know the process of getting him out of Afghanistan and to the U.S. for education. Derek could not have been more helpful. Unfortunately, he later left the U.S. Embassy to travel to other parts of the world, but he and I maintained internet contact throughout my stay in Afghanistan.

The process was not simple, but not impossible either, so we left with a pretty good feeling that we could accomplish this mission. In a perfect world, the mission would be a snap. This was not a perfect world, or mission, so we had our snap but also a couple of crackle and pops to go with it.

It was at this time I learned that Shoop and Wallace would be returning to the U.S. and leaving me behind to run the show. I had been taking a more active roll in the work of the academy, but never dreamed that I would be left alone to do this. You get used to having that security blanket of personnel with you and that was about to end. Their day for departure was coming rapidly.

"Who will be replacing you and when?" I asked.

"We are not sure who or when, but it could be a few weeks from now before you have a replacement."

The momentum had been established; I was being placed in charge of keeping the momentum going, and I was about to go from a three member team to a team of one. I was still a bit confused and concerned about the success rate of this mission. During our first briefing with Major General Weston, we were told we had no money. I had also been told by the General that there was no money or staff, so I basically had the feeling that I was being abandoned.

It reminded me of the movie "My Dog Skip." A young boy talks his parents into getting a dog that grows up with him through all the trials and tribulations of being a young boy and then a teenager. The boy, as well as the dog, gets into trouble, but throughout most of the movie, they stick together.

However, at the end of the movie, the boy leaves home on a train and the dog is left at the depot watching him go. I felt terrible for the dog. There is not a greater companion for forgiveness than a dog. I know it was just a movie, but it still was sad to see that type of ending.

Remember the prayer, "Dear Lord, let me try to be the person my dog thinks I am." I know I can't live up to that expectation, and I am not sure I have ever met anyone that could either.

While we had only been together for about six weeks, I felt we had grown very close and we had made significant progress. When they started planning their return trip, I was really saddened that I would be staying back. I did not yet feel comfortable in the roll I was about to assume. I felt like Skip the dog, and besides, I didn't even have any business cards! I asked Colonel Shoop and Lieutenant Colonel Wallace to watch the movie and pay close attention to the ending. I don't know if they ever watched it or not.

The big day arrived; we took pictures, and they departed for Bagram to begin their journey home. They were happy and I was happy for them, sort of. It had been a great start of a long mission, and now it was up to me to keep the snow ball rolling down the hill.

I grew to accept the short stay time as the norm for West Point personnel, as they would rotate in and out of Afghanistan on thirty to forty-five day cycles, with the exception of a few individuals. Because of such rotation standards, we could only work one piece of the puzzle at a time. One team would work the policy and doctrine, while the next could only work on the infrastructure, then another team worked assessment. It was important that we had just enough pieces of the puzzle completed by arrival time of the students. It was a great exercise in prioritizing tasks for a mission.

About five days after Shoop and Wallace departed, I got word that Colonel Ed Naessens would be arriving, bringing ideas, energy, and, most importantly, Snickers to Afghanistan. He had found out that I loved Snickers candy bars, so he had a load with him for us to savor during the time he was there. While Colonel Shoop and Lieutenant Colonel Wallace and I became very good friends, I probably became closer to Colonel Naessens than any other member of the West Point Team. This mission was about to become very exciting and fun.

FIRING POINT FOR RUSSIAN HIND HELICOPTERS

KFC KABUL

KITCHEN FOR MESS HALL

RICE ANYONE?

NMAA FLAG

R DAY WITH SMG GRANADO AND LTC NELSON

SHARIF GOLF SWING

SPEAKING AT CBT GRADUATION

THE SIGN

PURCHASING THE NMAA DOMAIN NAME

More than 13,000 photos were taken to document the extent of this mission. Photos included in this book were contributed by: MSG Joe Johnson and MAJ Fred Rice, OMC-A PAO, Colonels Chris King, Buck Buchanan, Ray Nelson, Barry Shoop, David Wallace, Ray Winkel, Lieutenant Colonel Doug Hays, and Dr. Larry Butler. Thank you for helping document one of the many outstanding missions in Afghanistan.

BUILDING THE
INFRASTRUCTURE

Another major issue we had to face was the actual building of the facilities. Initially, Qargha had been the choice location. Because of the devastation of the grounds from various conflicts, as well as redirection of funding for the security operations of the elections, the Qargha site would not be ready for opening in the timetable allowed. We wanted to have our cadets on site by February 2005.

As mentioned earlier, the initial members of the MAIST conducted site visits of the Kabul Military High School and the Afghanistan Air Academy to look for an alternate site. Lieutenant Colonel Donna Brazil and Major William Caruso, both of West Point, followed Forsythe and Neff, from January until February 2004. Based on a report signed by leaders of MoD, their mission was to serve as a bridge between the Military Academy Study Team and the work it conducted in October and November 2003, and the Military Academy Implementation Team that would be slated to stand up in June 2004 and would see the completion of the mission in 2005. The activities for site selection were basically dormant between February and June 2004. The liaison during that time frame was Lieutenant Colonel David Prugh, a West Point graduate who had volunteered for a tour in Afghanistan.

Lieutenant Colonel Prugh was assigned to establish the foundation of relationships that was to be carried over for the duration of our mission. One of his significant accomplishments was to have Major General Razak and his staff travel to West Point for tours and a briefing of the format used in training future officers. Because of that opportunity, everyone thought Major General Razak would become the first Superintendent of the National Military Academy of Afghanistan. No one thought it more than Major General Razak. Because of Lieutenant Colonel Prugh's work, the cooperation we had, especially from Major General Razak, was excellent.

Unfortunately Lieutenant Colonel Prugh was assigned to the Defense Operations Sector (DOS) for other missions of higher priority so we lost that valuable asset with the initial work of the academy. However, he did provide us with valuable information that helped our association with members of MoD. Also, Lieutenant Colonel Prugh was always available to visit with me when I had questions or concerns about how things were progressing. He departed before my mission was complete, but I can't help but think he indirectly kept in contact with the status of how we were progressing.

Colonel Shoop and Lieutenant Colonel Wallace had completed their work with the Policy and Doctrine documents and were now preparing to depart Kabul and return to West Point. However, before they left, we had to complete a ceremonial signing program with MoD personnel.

Brigadier General Amin, Colonel Shoop and I sat down at

MoD Headquarters and signed the policy and doctrine agreement that would establish the foundation as to how the academy would be operated. It was a great day for all involved. Shoop and Wallace had accomplished a significant component of the future of the academy while I rode along like an empty can tied to the bumper of a car that was speeding away with "Just Married" painted on the window. I admit: I was still somewhat oblivious as to what was really in store for me.

After Colonel Shoop and Lieutenant Colonel Wallace left and I had a few days to myself before the arrival of the next West Point faculty member, I was a bit uneasy as to his arrival, because I knew nothing about him. I was told that he had volunteered to come over early. I very much appreciated his eagerness and he would be an extremely valuable asset to the site development. I was later to realize that almost everyone that came to work on the academy from West Point had stepped up and volunteered for this mission.

Colonel Ed Naessens arrived with fire in his eyes and a touch of humor that made the job fun and exciting. I thought I was a bit off the wall with some of my humor, but Colonel Naessens put a whole new twist on our mission. He and I immediately bounded toward the mission at hand. There was no adjustment time for him. He came ready and willing to press forward to do whatever was needed to be done to make this mission successful.

Before he could officially come on board and pick up the mission, he had to in-process through all the basic stations at OMC-A. Added to the in-processing orientations of the base were options of "The Blue Collar Comedy Tour" and lessons in "Forty-two." Now we were ready to go.

Colonel Naessens had been one of the operation officers in 2001 when the U.S. forces fought the Taliban and displaced them out of Kabul and the surrounding mountain area. He brought that background of working with the Afghans to the table, and that experience was very instrumental in our discussions. We were now ready to start a new chapter in this saga.

The team now consisted of two-and-half people. I mention the one half person, Major Eric Arnoldus. He had been working with the Implementation Team along side of Lieutenant Colonel Prugh. He had also worked somewhat with Shoop and Wallace to help them transition into the mission. He was now being pulled back to DOS for other work. He was an extremely intelligent person that also provided us with valuable information. I wish he could have stayed on our team and I think he did too. We immediately started to plan our next step in the development of the academy.

The infrastructure was the next logical phase. It was imperative that we have some type of solid structure for the foundation of the academy. We needed to have this piece of the puzzle established and in place as soon as possible, along with logistically outlining where classrooms, labs, and accommodations for the cadets would be. We also had to have offices for faculty, and facilities for support personnel.

As we began our deliberations concerning the infrastructure, the Afghans brought up an earlier agreement that said the academy would be built in Qargha. An agreement had been signed by an earlier team, and they expected the United States to be true to their word.

I had a personal investment in not wanting the Qargha option. It may have been selfish, but I had taken a personal interest in this project. First, it would be impossible to complete the academy infrastructure by February 2005. Second, if we built in Qargha, then the project would still be in operation when my deployment time was up, and I would not get to see the mission completed. It was imperative that we find a site where the structures were fairly stable and we could get the academy off the ground. As I said, selfish, but it should be noted that leadership was changing with the U.S. forces on a monthly basis. As the changes happened, so did priorities, so I had a significant concern that if I left, the mission might be dropped for something of more importance to a new commander or chief.

I considered the building of the academy to be a new beginning for Afghanistan. The NMAA would be the birth of higher education that would benefit both the country and the military. There were other higher education institutions in Afghanistan, but nothing that would compare to the NMAA. The Afghans were starved for education, and as a result, the academy was not a hard sell to anyone at MoD or the Ministry of Higher Education. I started making references to the academy being "my baby," and that I wanted to be there when it was born. The Afghans liked that metaphor, and it seemed to motivate them to move forward each time I talked about the baby and its condition and delivery date.

Colonel Naessens and I spent a significant number of hours and days trying to convince MoD that the overall mission had changed since the time the earlier team's report had been completed. Each time we would meet with a different group of people, the same issues relating to what had been agreed on with people who had been there before us would be raised.

I found out later that not everything that was said to have been agreed on had even been discussed. It was important that I be in contact with the personnel who had preceded me, so I would not be "blindsided" by something that actually did not happen. It was also very helpful that Colonel Naessens had been briefed in great detail by earlier team members from West Point before coming over so that he brought that knowledge-base with him. It certainly did not hurt that Colonel Barney Forsythe, who was back at West Point, coordinated future personnel. It was extremely important that we remain in contact with him, because he had written the initial study.

Colonel Forsythe also realized that the mission was a moving target and objectives would have to be adjusted if this mission was to be successful. It was great to have that trust in the background; someone that is doing everything from providing data to being the head cheerleader.

I also learned very quickly that my best on-the-spot resource was Dr. Sardar. He had been with this project from the very beginning, and could tell Colonel Naessens and me when MoD might be trying to posture itself for a better deal than had been originally agreed on.

While all this was going on, we were coming under occasional rocket attacks. The area I was in was not a "lawless town" with fighting going on like you would see in the movies. However, it was necessary that we had to always be on guard of anything out of the ordinary. Everyone was always a bit suspicious of possible IED's and/or suicide bombers.

Colonel Naessens and I would be walking in the compound at night and would occasionally see a rocket going overhead that had originated from the mountains or just outside Kabul, and would randomly land somewhere on the other side of the city. There were times, though, that the rockets would hit very close to our compound.

One night in particular, Colonel Naessens and I were working at the office and an incoming rocket hit just outside our compound. The warning alarm erupted and we headed for our bunker. Colonel Naessens had only been there a few days, so I wanted to make sure that he was safe and out of harm's way.

After getting in our bunker, I looked around and noticed there was no Colonel Naessens. No one had seen him, and actually, most would not have recognized him, since he just arrived and had not been wearing his uniform.

I scrambled out of the bunker and ran back to our office only to find Colonel Naessens gone. Stepping out of the office I shouted, "Colonel Naessens!"

"I'm around the corner," was his reply.

I ran around the corner and there he is on the roof with his camera.

"What do you think you are doing?"

"I want to get a picture of the next incoming rocket."

"Have you lost your mind? We need to get in the bunker."

"But this will be a really cool picture."

At this point I learned the persuasive techniques of Colonel

Ed Naessens. I was not able to talk him into getting into the bunker, and he was able to convince me that an incoming rocket picture would be very cool. So I went back to the office and got my camera and we sat on the roof of the building waiting for the next rocket in hopes that one of us would get a photo. Talk about bonding. That was a great experience getting to know each other. We also agreed that neither one of us would qualify to be in the military intelligence branch of the Army. Fortunately, no other rockets came in so, no harm, no foul.

It is sad to say though that a rocket attack would have to happen to break-up the boredom of our daily meetings. Regardless of what happened in the evenings though, we had to be up and running the next morning. We had to get the Afghans off the Qargha location and into the mindset of someplace else. That someplace else had to be the Air Academy. We had to convince MoD that we had to move not because of the devastation at Qargha but because of time and completing the mission before I redeployed back to the United States. We had to take a different angle for the move. We chose the "Crown Jewel" option.

It was important that we sold the Air Academy location as the site, because the foundation of the buildings was basically intact. There was a lot of work that needed to be done, but it was not an impossible mission like the one we originally had. We went to MoD with the following rationale:

> The Air Academy would make a great location for the National Military Academy of Afghanistan because:
>
> The initial buildings, which included administration, feeding, and classrooms are basically intact.
>
> It is on the same property where Kabul International Airport is located, so it could be a very secure environment as well as easy access to dignitaries that would fly in to Kabul International Airport.
>
> Because of its location, foreign personnel would come in and observe the success of the academy as well as hold confer-

ences on the grounds because of the state of the art internet we will be implementing and the easy access to the airport.

Funding for infrastructure is limited, so this is the obvious site to "Have the baby born."

You have no air force, so you can downsize your classes and consolidate your students at a single facility nearby, which was also on the Kabul Airport grounds.

Because of its location (close to an international airport) and the opportunities that are presented, this site and the academy will become the "Crown Jewel" of Afghanistan. The only limitation that you have will be your imagination, so dream the dream and then make the dream happen.

WHAT DO YOU SEE IN YOUR FUTURE?

Afghans are dreamers, and that holds a bright future for them in my mind. They were consistently looking at a brighter future for their country. They are one of the more optimistic groups of people I have ever met. I can walk down the street in the United States and ask ten people what they predict for the future, and I truly believe that eight out of ten would see our future to be bleak and not in good standing.

In Afghanistan, I purposely would walk up to strangers and visit with them about the future of Afghanistan and I usually got a completely different response. Some of my American friends would say they were just trying to please me. If that was the case, then it worked. I consistently heard comments about a positive future and bright outlook on life. They, to the person, said that they needed the support of the coalition forces. Not just the United States, but from everyone. If more countries had that attitude, I think we would be in much better shape.

After much discussion, we finally convinced MoD to allow us to consider the Afghanistan Air Academy near Kabul International Airport for a future site. This was a very exciting time for Colonel Naessens and me. However, we still had several barriers to break down before we could get into the full swing of reworking the infrastructure.

The Air Academy was still occupied by faculty and a few students in class. We were going to have to extract them from the site so we could begin reconstruction of the facilities. There was also a significant amount of equipment from previous courses that had been taught and would have to be removed. The Afghans don't seem to throw away anything. They are very innovative in using spare parts of a piece of equipment to get a completely different piece of machinery to work.

If I were in charge of getting rid of that equipment, I would have sold it on Ebay. I think I could have eliminated Afghanistan's debt and totally eradicated the opium crops because of the souvenirs that could be available for purchase. Everyone would become wealthy!

We had missiles, anti-aircraft guns, Soviet helmets, training charts, Soviet aircraft and tanks, just to name a few of the items. It should be noted that the weapons would be cut down to pieces and sold as a scrap from the war. There would be an etching that indicated this was from a certain soviet tank from the Russian/Afghan War. To sell missiles, anti-aircraft guns, and tanks in complete and working order on Ebay would raise to a record level the proponents for gun control, so that would not be an option.

It was an Ebay customer's paradise. You name it, they had it. I know we are not to take any war trophies home with us, and I didn't, but it was hard not to consider the possibilities. Whoever figures out Ebay in that country can become a completely different type of warlord! That person will be at the top of the pyramid.

MY FRIEND, I WILL MAKE AN OFFER
YOU CANNOT REFUSE

The bottom line was that we had people and equipment on-site that needed to be removed. We also had to rebuild the infrastructure and have it ready for the opening on February 5, 2005. That was just nine months away, and we still had no money. It was marketing time for Wilhite and Naessens. We both felt if we could just get people to listen to our message, then we could polish this "Crown Jewel" and make it shine. We were up to the task; now we just needed targets of opportunity, and there were plenty of targets out there.

The first order of business was to determine where the money would come from. The United States had committed a significant amount of money to Operation Enduring Freedom, and we planned on getting some of it. We needed to find that source.

There were many facilities and roads being built all around the country. Recruiting centers, schools, hospitals, and roads were being showcased weekly. That process, under the guidance of Major General Weston, was as impressive as any major operation I had ever been involved with or even read about.

As the engineers worked their magic, they started completing their work under budget. That is where we were going to have to obtain our funding. We needed to grab the scraps that were not used in other projects. One special group of people that worked closely with the engineers was the Seabees.

This is where Chief Clint Rainey entered the picture. Chief Rainey was passionate about virtually every project in which he was involved. Colonel Naessens and I got to know this man both as a professional and a friend. We took Chief Rainey out to the future site of the academy and walked him through the dream that we had. We asked him to visualize this property four years from now, with the graduation class marching on the parade field in the horseshoe area around the dormitories. Walking through the old abandon buildings, we visualized where the administrative offices would be built, science classrooms with laboratories established, a dining facility that would serve a large number of cadets at one time, security facilities, dormitories for cadets, computer rooms, regular classrooms, a future superintendent's quarters, heating and air conditioning, and, last but not least, latrines (bathrooms) with running water!

Chief Rainey's eyes would get bigger and bigger as we described our pipedream. His voice would also get animated when talking about how we could make this happen. It was Chief Rainey that had supervised the building of many facilities and had a good idea of just how much it would cost to make this academy a reality. This was a mission that no one expected to become successful, and we had just found the person that could do the impossible: find bits and pieces of money from the engineering pool, convince his superiors of the importance of this mission, and begin staging funding for future work.

There were a couple of minor hurdles that Colonel Naessens and I had to deal with before we could start soliciting bids on rebuilding the infrastructure. We still had personnel and equipment we had to extract before rebuilding could take place.

In order for this change to take place Colonel Naessens and I agreed that if we didn't have the support from the MoD, all our efforts would be wasted. We decided to work backwards and start from the top selling our program.

We already knew MoD had agreed to the academy, so that was not the issue. The issue was to move the site from the original location of Qargha to the old air academy by the airport. In order to accomplish our objectives, we had to take our biggest obstacle, time, and use it to our advantage.

We went to the various departments in MoD and pitched our story. We only had nine months to have the academy ready to accept students. This is where I conjured up the concept of the "Baby" as representing the academy. If we were to have a successful delivery, then we must make special arrangements for the birth of the academy.

We even had a special name for the academy. While it was called officially the National Military Academy of Afghanistan, we had reduced it to the acronym NMAA. We pronounced the NMAA, Knee-Ma. They liked the name of our new baby and immediately picked up on that title.

We told MoD that time was not on our side, but we had a

solution. The Afghans like solutions, especially if it is presented to them and they don't have to be involved in a series of meetings to discuss, debate, or make a decision.

- Move the academy site from Qargha to the old air academy.

- Allow the current classes at the air academy to be completed before extraction so as to not disrupt training. That would give us time to draw up plans for reworking the infrastructure.

- That would also give us time to find funding for the work that needed to be done.

- Extract the personnel and relocate them to another air academy that was being commanded by a Lieutenant General who was also a Russian Cosmonaut.

- Identify the Superintendent of the academy and get him on board as soon as possible.

- Start the initial process of identifying the essential personnel needed to get the academy started.

- Draw up a plan of action that would indicate what infrastructure would need to be completed at the air academy site.

It was hard for the MoD personnel to disagree with Colonel Naessens and me. We were so enthusiastic about the mission that they got swept up in the excitement. We never let on that there was a problem with money to complete the change. The issue we continually pushed was "time." We did not have time to build it from scratch, and I emphasized to anyone that would listen that I would not return to the United States with my last mission being incomplete. Besides, no one was really pushing me from our higher headquarters because they had bigger issues to deal with. I had been told this was a "nice-to-do thing" from the beginning. During this time, I didn't think too many people thought the National

Military Academy of Afghanistan (NMAA) would even begin, much less become a reality.

Colonel Naessens went so far as to design the patch that the faculty and students would be wearing that distinguished the academy from other military units. He started making a drawing of the symbol for certificates that reflected the NMAA. He was definitely a dreamer with a vision. It is not hard to get caught up in the moment when you have people like that.

We felt our biggest obstacle related to the general officers that were stationed at the academy. One was in charge of the air force training and the other was in charge of the school that taught maintenance for the aircraft. While I don't remember the air force training general, I do remember Major General Razak that headed the maintenance program.

Major General Razak was a tall, distinguished gentleman that Colonel Naessens and I grew to respect and appreciate quickly during our time with him. General Razak had been to the United States and toured The United States Military Academy at West Point, and had his picture pasted all over the *New York Times*. Everyone at West Point thought he was going to be selected as the superintendent of the academy. He believed that too. As a result, once we had been through the MoD personnel and had their support, then the support from General Razak was not a problem.

General Razak helped us convince the other general officer to make the move. Getting him and his staff to nicer accommodations was not as difficult as we initially thought. It also didn't hurt to have MoD Education Minister Fawzi supporting us in the move. He came over and held a meeting that was basically one sided. He brought everyone in, told them what was going to happen, and then left. Shortly afterward, it happened. The air force general officer, his staff, and faculty disappeared.

General Razak was pleased that his people were getting to complete their courses, so basically Colonel Naessens and I were given free access to anyplace on the academy grounds. General Razak would join us on many of these walks. We would daydream and plant visions of the academy of the future and how the students, under his leadership, would have a significant impact on his country for many years to come. What he would be in charge of would be the education and future of Afghanistan, both in the military as well as the civilian sector. General Razak would smile and nod his head approvingly.

It was at this time that both Colonel Naessens and I thought his baby might actually be born. Never mind that we still had no money. Afghans are noted for their dreaming, and, as stated earlier, they were always optimistic about their future. Colonel Naessens and I got caught up on that dream and, therefore, failing to develop an academy for the country would not be an option. Maintaining that enthusiasm throughout was, at times, a tested commodity. We were still in the minority that thought we would be successful.

Like two kids playing in a toy store, Colonel Naessens and I went through each building taking notes as to what needed to be removed and what needed to be fixed. We had five initial buildings for faculty, staff, students, and classrooms. These five buildings had forty-four rooms each in them. The superintendent's office would be in the administrative building along with the department heads and faculty for the academy. The administration building was off-set from the students' quarters.

The students' quarters were four buildings formed in a horse-shoe shape configuration that was fronted by a covered reviewing platform and a hard-top parade area. We forecasted the buildings would house the students as well as classrooms. The first building, nearest the administration building, would be designated as the first facility that was to be readied for the cadet basic training, which was to be held the first part of February. It was extremely important that its building be completed above all others, including the administrative building. The remaining buildings in the horseshoe would be completed after the grand opening, which was slated after Cadet Basic Training, during the latter part of March.

A sixth building was the dining facilities (DFAC) for the students. That building was already in place, but had to have a significant amount of work done on it to make it appealing to students, faculty, and the many visitors we projected would be joining us as they visited the NMAA.

Colonel Naessens went through all the facilities and designed a plan that basically indicated where each student would be staying, where classes would be located, where faculty and tactical officers would be housed, and how the dining facility would be reworked. In other words, he put together a power point presentation that was as impressive as anything done for the academy development.

Colonel Naessens also forecasted the next four years, including the new students' population and additional work that needed to be done for the expansion of the academy. That was just one of the many presentations that he prepared that helped get the snowball rolling down the hill. Excitement was growing in the MoD, as well as the NMAA future site. The enthusiasm was not quite as fervid at the U.S. base. Many thought it was still a pipedream that was unrealistic. They didn't know about our secret weapon of Chief Rainey and the magic he was working in the background.

NAY! NAY! MINES!

Security was always an issue with the academy. Early on we were concerned that the academy would make a good target for opposing forces, and to have a catastrophic event happen would destroy anything we were trying to build. Colonel Naessens decided to take my GPS and chart out the perimeters of the academy so we could put up some type of wall to keep control of the activities that would be taking place during the school year.

Fortunately, General Razak accompanied us on one of the walking tours around the perimeter. As we got to certain locations, Colonel Naessens would record the GPS Latitude and Longitude of the property and mark it on a makeshift map for future reference. This was a bit different than what Razak had been used to. I believe if you asked him to give you the perimeter layout of the academy, he would have pointed with his finger and said, "Over there, over there, and over there." We wanted to be more precise than that.

On one particular area, as I walked toward a corner boundary to mark, I heard General Razak scream, "Wilhite, nay, nay, nay!"

I stopped walking, turned to General Razak and said, "What?"

"Mines!"

I had just walked into a mine field that had been laced round the academy perimeter. I looked at Colonel Naessens, and while backing up, he was looking at me and going for his camera.

"Ed, this is not another photo opportunity!"

He had already taken a picture of an unexploded mortar round that I had stepped over on one occasion and was still disappointed in not getting a picture of the incoming rockets at our base camp. The man loved to take pictures.

I slowly retraced my steps out of the mine field and we carefully walked the remainder of the outer wall, taking our finger and pointing to, "Over there, over there, and over there." I guess General Razak wasn't as removed from the technology aspect as we originally thought.

During the briefings we had with our chief of OMC-A, Major General Weston, the academy portion would report that we were continuing to meet with MoD personnel and Major General Razak. We were hesitant to go into any detail about the planning and implementation stage of the academy because of the length of the meetings. These meetings, with the "big boys," included everything going on in the country. We didn't need to get shot down by someone that basically did not have a clue as to what we were doing. We would save that for a small group meeting with only Colonel Naessens, Dr. Sardar, myself, and Major General Weston.

However, during one briefing with the "Big Boys," the head of the engineers, Commander Orlasky announced to MG Weston that there was money available for the NMAA. Other projects had come under budget and our hero, Chief Rainey, had convinced Commander Orlasky to channel the surplus to the academy. We had approximately five hundred thousand dollars for the academy.

Remember we initially had a sixty-five million dollar budget, and it went down to zero. We now had five hundred thousand dollars that was available for the NMAA. Five hundred thousand is only .7% of the initial funding we had, but it was a start! That amount slowly grew to one million dollars, then 1.7 million, and we started to believe this mission might work. As other projects were also coming in under budget, the extra funding would be channeled to the academy. Yes, the Army has done that on occasion. The engineers had bought in on the National Military Academy of Afghanistan and were redirecting surplus funds to help our cause. We saw it grow slowly but steadily.

During one briefing, I informed the General that I could begin the academy on a four million dollar budget. I concluded that if I had to have a bake sale and sell cupcakes at the weekly bazaar to raise the money, then I would do it. Major General Weston wanted to know how many cupcakes I would have to sell and I said, "Only one, but I am asking four million dollars for it!" The four million was quite a drop from the original sixty-five million identified for the NMAA, but, based on the input from Commander Orlasky and Chief Rainey, we concluded that we could give birth to the NMAA on that sum.

The presentation that Colonel Naessens developed for Major General Weston really tilted the budget in our favor. I have to admit that prior to this particular presentation, I had reservations that we would actually complete this mission. I was still not convinced that anybody really cared if we completed the NMAA or not. We were still off in a little spot of paradise on Kabul Compound and no one bothered to check on us. As I reflect on that time, the "not bothered us" was probably one of the most important things we had going for us. We didn't get drug down in other "Administrivia."

Occasionally we would be sidetracked with other issues. To some people the issues might pose a problem. For Colonel Naessens and myself, it was welcome because it broke up the endless meetings we were having. Did I tell you I hate meetings?

One particular issue related to computers. We received notice that West Point was sending computers to Afghanistan for the academy. Colonel Naessens was aware the shipment would take place. He just didn't know exactly when it would arrive.

These were older computers that West Point was replacing, and they thought sending them to Afghanistan would be a great gesture to help set up the NMAA. That was a great gesture, with one exception; we didn't have electricity but one hour per day, and we didn't know what time of day we would receive it.

When I first heard about the shipment, I thought someone had lost their mind. Colonel Naessens assured me that was not the case. Somehow, we would need a solution to get the electricity. First things first though: we had to go inventory the containers that were coming in.

We arrived at an old warehouse, and to my amazement, there were about thirty huge containers to be inventoried. We spent the next week going through each container and counting every piece of equipment that arrived. We had a shipping document, but we had to double check the contents. Colonel Naessens made a list as to where everything would go and how it would be used. We had the help of some Afghan workers that were very appreciative of our efforts. I think it was the first time they had seen individuals of our rank jump into the middle of a project and help out. In the past they had always done the dirty work. We were able to remove each computer and count each one by serial number. The materials also included wiring, hard drives, and just about anything you would need to set up shop. After the inventory was completed, we stored the equipment until we could get the academy rebuilt and electricity established. Now it was back to the academy area for follow-up work.

We took the inventoried information to MoD and excitedly shared it with Minister Wardak and the others. When we were talking about the electricity, Colonel Naessens quickly replied, "No problem, sir, we will get electricity!" I thought he was going to get a standing ovation for his comments. Again, the dreams were happening and the vision was starting to come into focus. We now had to get the word out to people beyond the Ministry of Defense. That became our next step that we could work on with almost immediate results.

Communications were less than stellar in Afghanistan, but it was important that our message of the academy be advertised. Between the computers and classrooms, we had to determine the process of recruiting the top students in Afghanistan plus an assessment process that would be fair and represent the ethnic groups of the country.

Colonel Naessens and I developed an admissions flyer for the Recruiting Assistance Team (RAT) visits. With the support of Lieutenant Colonel Clint Dawson, that information started getting out around the country. The RAT helped develop recruiting stations around the country to assist in assessing and signing up Afghan citizens into the Afghan National Army (ANA). Lieutenant Colonel Dawson's success was remarkable. His team was attending opening ceremonies on a weekly basis all over the country. Their support in getting out the word to the recruiters was just what we needed.

We also needed faculty and staff personnel. Colonel Naessens and I reviewed and recommended significant changes that were part of an augmentation plan for the academy. It included faculty, staff, support personnel like cooks, cleaning, guards, etc. They had to be phased in and priorities had to be addressed as to who would be first hires, etc. We concluded Superintendent, administration, faculty deans, and department heads would be the first hires for the NMAA.

We then had to look at equipment needs. We had nothing, I mean nothing for equipment. We started to scrounge sites all over Kabul and found desks and chairs at various storage locations. Never in my life did I do so much swapping and trading. I felt like I was in a bad movie with no script. At that time though, it was all we had to work with. We would work daily as though we had our students lined up in the wings and waiting to come on board. We had to move forward with this mission, reminding ourselves that failure was not an option. As the Afghans said, "Inshallah," which means, "It's God's will." Colonel Naessens and I found ourselves making that statement more often than we cared to realize. At times, we both felt "Inshallah" was all we had to support us.

Adding fuel to the fire was the initial work up of the Program of Instruction (POI) for Cadet Basic Training (CBT). Colonel Naessens had some experience with his work as an Operations Officer in 2001 when the U.S. drove the Taliban out of Afghanistan, so he was familiar with the needs of soldiers in Afghanistan. We both knew the CBT handbook would be changed dramatically, but it still needed to be laid out for consideration. We later did make some radical changes because of supplies, equipment, and training standards.

We also worked up a cadet schedule of courses for a four year period of study. Again, this changed as time got closer, but the foundation was extremely important to have as a working document. Our course of instruction was to include majors in engineering, and political science. Later we were to add foreign language to the mix. This baby had been conceived and was growing on a daily basis.

Colonel Naessens was also active in developing the process for sending textbooks to Afghanistan for translation into Dari. He had been working with Lieutenant Colonel Wallace concerning the legal ramifications of copyright infringements. The legality of such a process didn't seem to bother the Afghans. While they have lawyers in that country, they don't seem to get caught up in certain legal issues like we do in the U.S.

As mentioned earlier, Colonel Naessens developed the patch for the NMAA faculty, staff, and cadets to wear on their uniform for identification and recognition. Initially, the Afghans did not fully accept the concept, but as the opening started to get closer, they welcomed their new patch and wore it with pride. Colonel Naessens did an unbelievable amount of work while there, but I think he might be most proud of the patch he designed. This will be his legacy to the National Military Academy of Afghanistan.

Colonel Naessens was only there for a couple of months (July/August 2004) but as one can see, he worked tirelessly toward the mission of developing the NMAA. That was pretty standard for anyone that came over. Almost to the person, everyone that came over wanted to extend or come back. It is not often you can see success on a daily basis in a war zone, but it was happening to us and that made our work extremely enjoyable.

During the end of August, the rocket attacks became more frequent and Colonel Naessens was concerned about the follow-on team's arrival. He wrote to West Point and informed the next team not to come and he would stay. I think he was still trying to get a picture of a rocket. His request was denied by his boss, and he was told to start preparing for his redeployment back to the United States.

Colonel Naessens met one last time with General Razak and they exchanged gifts, which is customary, and Colonel Naessens left the academy site with the feeling that Razak was going to become our first superintendent of the NMAA.

At the end of August, Colonel Naessens returned to West Point and was replaced by three of the most interesting people I have ever met. These individuals would play a major role in the hiring and selection of faculty for the NMAA, as well as training recruiters to help identify potential cadets around the country.

Colonel Ray Winkel, Head of the Physics Department and Colonel Naessens's boss, was one of the new personnel. Now I knew why Colonel Naessens's request to stay was rejected. Colonel Gary Krahn, Head of the Math Department, and Dr. Larry Butler, Professor, Physical Education Department arrived to work on the next piece of the puzzle. The intensity picked up like never before. All of a sudden it started to appear that someone other than the Afghans was starting to notice our work. As my father used to say, "It's now time to fish or cut bait!"

RECRUITING IN
AFGHANISTAN

(STUDENTS AND FACULTY)

The first day Colonel Winkel, Colonel Krahn, and Dr. Butler were in the compound, we had an IED (Improvised Explosive Devise) detonate just outside our perimeter. Colonel Krahn and I were visiting and he said, "When is the last time you had 'BOOM!' an attack?"

"About one second ago," was my reply.

We looked outside my office and saw a large black mushroom cloud coming up just outside of the gate on the west side of the compound. Alarms went off and everyone headed for the bunkers. I had not yet even told Krahn, Winkel, and Butler where the bunkers were.

This incident was the first one where I actually saw people killed via an IED. The bomb went off by a security facility killing two Americans, three Nepalese, and two Afghan children. The bodies were brought to the medical facility at Kabul Compound, which was next to my accommodations. I witnessed two specific issues that evening: death and watching a group of young National Guard soldiers from Florida working security grow up from boys to men as they fanned out across Kabul attempting to find the people responsible for the explosion.

Morris Massey might refer to experiences like that as a "Significant Emotional Event." That is exactly what it was. Not only for me, but for a large number of soldiers that, up to this time, had patrolled in the surrounding city and had not seen much action.

The bodies were processed and we had to move forward and try to get this horror out of our minds. We did move forward, but the vision I had that evening will never leave me. Only a soldier or individuals in the police or fire department realize the nature of the dangers they face while trying to conduct their mission. While their work may seem calm and sometimes boring, they must always be on alert for possible situations to turn chaotic or even deadly. In our case we had just had a deadly situation but had to continue with our next step in the process and we did not have the time to reflect on the situation at hand. It was a reminder though that we were in a war zone and need to be ever alert of the environment around us. What was next?

FACULTY AND STAFF

Up to this point, we had written the policy and doctrine and initial work had begun on the infrastructure of the academy. However, we were still missing a few pieces of the puzzle. We did not have a superintendent, faculty, recruiting team, or students. This phase was to present some of the highest and lowest times of the development of the NMAA.

In the United States we seem to be hung up on time and deadlines. True, many of us put off some of our work until the deadline gets really close. Then we put a significant amount of pressure on ourselves to produce an acceptable product. That is just not the case in Afghanistan. Timelines do not seem to faze the leadership. When leadership is ready to make a decision, it can come quickly. But it is pretty much on their schedule, not ours.

Our problem was finding the appropriate leader to make decisions. Once we did find the appropriate personnel, we were able to obtain the results we were looking for. This bit of information became part of our briefing for the West Point personnel that would be incoming in the next few rotations. No one actually told me this bit of valuable information. I had to learn it on my own, along with the West Point personnel who were there from Colonel Naessens to the next rotation.

It was important that we had an Afghan leader that was intelligent and committed to the NMAA. All along we thought General Razak was going to be selected as the first Superintendent. He was part of the planning committee, had traveled to the U.S. and to West Point to observe how the United States Military Academy operates, was the commander of the Air University on the grounds we had identified, and had received approval for starting the NMAA. Everything just seemed to fit in place for him to be the selection.

Colonel Winkel, Krahn, and Dr. Butler had met General Razak while he was at West Point and were looking forward to seeing him again. The meeting was joyous and very friendly. We were all motivated to get moving with additional work for the academy.

One morning, the four of us were called to the academy for a meeting and the announcement of the Superintendent for the NMAA. We were excited to just go through the formalities and then begin the celebration with General Razak. When we arrived we were told that General Razak would not be in attendance. We all thought that was a bit strange, but this was Afghanistan and they have their appointments a bit differently than we do. We were then told General Razak would not be the commander. Another selection had been made. The new Superintendent of the National Military Academy of Afghanistan was Major General Mohammad Sharif.

General Sharif had been a former Northern Alliance Commander during the fall of the Taliban and currently was the Chief of Staff of a post near Kabul. To say we were shocked at the selection is a total understatement. I had no idea who this man was, and more importantly, I now had to deal with General Razak, because we were going to have to remove him from his facility to make way for the new commander. Also, the Air Force General that had not completely departed the grounds heard of the decision and decided he did not have to move, so he planted himself back in his old office and would not budge. This was a major road block for us; getting these two individuals out of their offices and off the academy grounds without them killing each other or someone else. This was another challenge that we were not prepared for. The Air Force General did not like General Razak and wasn't too thrilled about having us there either, so his removal had to be very diplomatic.

Colonel Winkel, Colonel Krahn, Dr. Butler, and I met with Razak and expressed our sorrow that he would not be the first Superintendent of the NMAA. We really worked on the positives that he had already done to lay the foundation and the important contribution he would be able to make for the future of Afghanistan in other ways. I really think he took it as smoke being blown up his uniform, but relented and gave up his location to move to another site. I have thought about General Razak a lot since that time. I know his pride was injured, but he was a team player and did not interfere with us moving forward. I also did not know what he was promised if he moved, but he must have been very satisfied.

The Air Force General was another matter though. We had to call in the big guns from MoD, Minister of Education Fawzi, and he brought everyone together, from Razak to the Air Force General and both their staffs and told them to vacate the property as soon as possible. He even told them when possible was.

Minister Fawsi said, "You will start vacating your offices now, and will be completely out by the end of the day tomorrow."

With that simple statement, he got up and walked out. Everyone understood what he meant though, and it was not a time for discovery or inquiry learning. As the Nike commercial says, "Just do it!" And they did. They immediately started the process. Not happy campers, but "The Leader" had spoken and they did not question his authority.

I'M NOT TAKING THIS JOB. NO WAIT, YES I AM!

While the two generals were planning their move, we got a phone call indicating General Sharif was not going to accept the position. Now we are without a leader again and we have just kicked the other leaders off the property. We had not even met General Sharif yet and he was giving up on us. The four of us drove over to MoD to find out what was going on and to determine what our next plan of action would be. At this time, we did not need distracters or delays. The NMAA was scheduled to open in about five months and I was not going to let that date slide. People were already telling me we should delay its opening, but I refused to have it as a "Mission Incomplete." I kept pressing everyone to make decisions and to continue pushing the snowball down the hill.

About as quickly as we heard General Sharif had refused the position, we heard that he had reconsidered the appointment and was now coming on board as Superintendent. We visited with Major General Murad Ali, the Minister of Personnel, and asked him what had happened and why did General Sharif change his mind. The only answer we were given was, "I stimulated him to reconsider." In that country, you have no idea what that actually meant. We were just glad to have someone on board. That evening we had fun brainstorming stimulation techniques that might have been used to convince General Sharif to reconsider. I don't know if any of them would have actually been used, but it was fun to bounce around options.

INTRODUCTION OF THE FIRST SUPERINTENDENT OF THE NMAA

A day or two later we were asked to return to MoD and meet General Sharif. He was a rather short, stocky person with dark eyes and a beard. I still didn't know what stimulation he had received, but he was saying all the right words and was ready to start moving forward with the building of the academy. Hindsight says the selection was very good, because he was not afraid to stand up to the chain of command and he was concerned about the success of the academy, its personnel, and students. That was determined early on. He agreed that we needed to select our initial faculty and to start looking at department heads for the primary offices. We also told him that after these individuals were selected, we would step back and become advisors to the department heads and assist them with their selections, keeping in mind we were looking for 'best qualified,' and not their buddies.

THE SNOWBALL STARTS DOWN THE HILL

The essential list of objectives was starting to mount up. We had to recruit and interview faculty for the academy and, at the same time, establish a recruiting and assessment format for the potential students we would be receiving. While maintaining that momentum, we also had to stay in favor with the Corps of Engineers so they could get the bids finalized and we could begin renovation of the facilities.

It was the latter part of September and the opening was approximately 150 days away. We had about two and one half million dollars as seed money to begin our work. With another five hundred thousand, we felt we could actually start and complete the first year of academics with the bare minimum materials. This would be no more or less than other institutions. At Kabul University Engineering Library, we were shown there was not one single book available. The Taliban had destroyed all those books during their reign of terror.

Colonel Winkel and Dr. Butler headed up the initial review of potential faculty candidates and would do a screening of the final ones for positions with the academy. Colonel Krahn and I set about establishing a training program and plan for the recruiting of the students around Afghanistan. I don't think any of us had an idea of what we were about to get ourselves into. It was high speed from the beginning and never did slow down.

Colonel Winkel and Dr. Butler did a review of over fifteen hundred applicants that had been provided by the MoD Personnel Office. They also received over two hundred additional applications for individuals that were not on the MoD list but were friends of friends of friends, etc. Very few, if any, were actually qualified, but Winkel and Butler reviewed them just to appease certain MoD personnel.

They were looking for primary leaders in fields such as physical training, language, computers, history, physics, math, etc. From that extensive list, the four of us interviewed approximately 200 individuals for twenty-five positions. The cultural education I received during the interviews was better than any humanities class I could have ever received in a university. It was tiring and gruesome doing the interviews, but we learned so much about the educational background of the individuals we were interviewing. We could not help but be excited each day as we met with the candidates and anxiously awaited their answers to our questions.

Many had been involved in the Afghan/Russian war as well as the tribal and Taliban conflicts, so their current knowledge-base relating to educational changes was somewhat weak. Many had also received advanced degrees in Russia. Before the Russian invasion, many Afghan soldiers attended universities in Moscow and other cities. That relationship, however, was terminated with the invasion in the 1980's. Now we are involved with the Afghans, their objectives, and concerns. Not everyone in Afghanistan wanted us there. I was concerned that we, too, would eventually be called invaders, and, as a result, our relationship could be soured and we could end up fighting the Afghans and not fighting in support of the Afghans. I hoped not.

Knowledge was important, but it seemed to be not as important as ethnic balance, which came back to haunt us for a brief period of time. After completing about half the interviews, Dr. Butler and I went to Minister of Defense Wardak and told him that if we were to get the best leaders for the academy then ethnic balance might have to be waived for this particular situation. He was in agreement with that, but there were multiple stumbling blocks that we faced through our own chain of command. There have been some writings that a particular ethnic group or another would be selected for leadership positions. I can say that while I was there, Major General Weston would not let that happen, and his belief of ethnic balance was paramount in establishing a smoother running government. The hiring of the faculty might have been the only exception that I was aware of. Even with the hiring, we tried to maintain the ethnic balance as best we could. A plan of action was put in place to educate people in the future who were not being represented in the department head selection process. Remember, we started with twenty-five faculty. That would quickly grow to two hundred-fifty and then to five hundred, if the academy continued to grow like we were planning.

As we continued to interview candidates, we noticed some of the strange answers that were given to us. A significant number of candidates were not aware the United States was involved in World War II, because they had been educated in Russia, and for some strange reason, they left out the U.S. involvement in the War.

However, Dr. Butler takes first place with one of his interview experiences. He asked an individual who wanted to be considered for the Department Head of History to name a leader from the

United States that he was familiar with. The individual's eyes lit up and he said, "Yes, your former president, Abraham Clinton." I missed that president in my history books, as did Dr. Butler, so the gentleman was asked to tell Dr. Butler and Colonel Winkel about former President Abraham Clinton. The candidate said, "He freed the slaves, but had an affair!" He was not selected.

For at least a week, Colonel Winkel and Dr. Butler made up one team while Colonel Krahn and I made up a second team. We conducted interviews during the day and then at night evaluated our scores and selected the top twenty-five leadership positions. After the positions were all agreed upon, we submitted them to our personnel at higher headquarters and fought the battles that followed about ethnic balance. We had convinced MoD, but we did not realize the roadblocks that would be presented by the American chain of command. It caught us off guard. There was such a concern about the ethnic balance that quality of leadership could have easily been put aside. We told our chain of command, "You can have good educational leaders as department heads or you can have ethnic balance. You can't have both."

It was a known fact that because of educational opportunities offered to select ethnic groups and denied to others, there would be a skew in the educational balance in a manner that was unacceptable. That being said, we just had to convince everyone this would have to be an "exception to policy."

At night, while in bed trying to go to sleep, I would reflect on the day's actions. There were times I would think the United States was not that far removed from Afghanistan in its educational opportunities for the ethnic, religious, or gender population. While some groups call those missed opportunities for advancement the "Glass Ceiling," others call it what it really is: "Discrimination." Regardless of what it is called, we are guilty of such actions.

I also started to get a feeling that the leadership at Kabul compound was beginning to show some interest in our work. People wanted to get involved in actions about which they were clueless. As a result, we started getting blocked in our progress from both sides. This was very disturbing. If it were not for having a three member team from West Point at this particular time, the mission would have been scratched. There were just too many internal battles to fight for one or two people.

To add to the already hectic schedule that was developing, I got word that our Afghan high school student Shoiab Yosoufzai was to catch a flight almost immediately for the United States to start his prep program at the University of Nebraska, Omaha, and I had a limited amount of time to get him to the airport.

I had already experienced problems getting him from Kabul to Islamabad to get a visa for travel to the United States. He had been arrested in Islamabad and had to bribe the police to keep from going to jail. I had given him one hundred and fifty dollars in case of an emergency, and the police took all of that money. One hundred and fifty dollars is what a school teacher would make in four months teaching, so it was a lot of money.

He had safely returned and eventually got his visa. We then had to get his ticket to go to Dubai, then onto the United States. I told Shoiab to pack his bags and be ready for a quick departure, but little did I know he was going to be going as quickly as he did.

I had his departure scheduled to go on a Friday. I was told not to buy the ticket until the day before he was to depart. Based on previous experiences in this country, I thought I would double check a couple of days out and see about purchasing a ticket just in case there might be a problem. There was!

At 8:30 Wednesday morning, I called the ticket office and was informed the particular airlines we were going to take had been grounded and would not be in operation for at least another month. There was only one other airline to fly to Dubai, and it was nicknamed "Inshallah Airlines," which means "If Allah wishes" or "If Allah wills." Not a reliable airline, but it was the only one we had contact with.

I rushed to the ticket office to see what the schedule was; at the same time, I sent word out to try to find Shoiab. He was not at home, but was somewhere en route to Kabul University. I did find out that his bags were packed.

At the ticket office, I pleaded with the agent to get me as much information as possible. I explained this was an extremely important trip for this young man and he had dealt with many hurdles to get to this point and I desperately needed his assistance.

He informed me that the next and last flight was to depart in thirty minutes from Kabul International and it looked like Shoiab was going to miss his chance to go to the United States and eventually enroll at the United States Military Academy.

The ticket official saw the drop of my spirit and told me he would see what he could do. He picked up the phone and made a call. I listened intently, even though I did not have a clue as to what the conversation was. After a couple of minutes he smiled said, "Tashakur" and hung up the phone.

The official looked at me and said, "My friend, the plane will not take off for ninety minutes."

"That is an extra hour. Is there a problem?" I inquired.

"No, they are holding it for you"

"Who is? The airline company?"

"No, I have a friend in the control tower that owes me a favor and he is holding the plane."

"Great! Now I need to buy a ticket." I was extremely relieved, but only for a short time.

"My friend, I cannot sell you a ticket for this airline. You will have to go to another location."

He told me the location and Masoom, our other translator, Colonel Winkel, and I departed to the seediest part of Kabul. We would have never made it without Masoom.

We got the ticket and headed straight for the airport as quickly as we could. We did not know if Shoiab had been found or not. We arrived at the airport and I found Colonel Hamdullah, Shoiab's dad, Major General Sharif, and another military officer there waiting on us. Shoiab had been found and was on his way to the airport.

We got him on the plane and I saluted it as it flew over our compound, wondering what would happen next to Shoiab. The time was ten o'clock in the morning when he flew over. The entire ordeal took less than one and one half hours.

With Shoiab having to leave a day early, we now had another problem. He was to get in Dubai one day early and there would be no one there to meet him and take care of his flight from Dubai to the United States. There was a point of contact, but he did not know Shoiab would arrive a day early. Lieutenant Colonel Dale Brown and I drove to the U.S. Embassy and tried to make contact with someone who could help us contact the contact in Dubai. Sound confusing? It was as confusing as it sounded at this point.

I was confronted by a lady in an office who wanted to know what we were doing there. When I explained to her what was going on, she responded that it sounded like a personal problem to her, and immediately kicked us out of her office. She said it was not the embassy's role to take care of the Army personnel. They took care of the Marines, but only because they guarded the embassy. Lieutenant Colonel Brown thought my head was going to explode.

Fortunately, before she arrived, I had made friends with an individual in the embassy that took care of contacting our Dubai individual, and three days later Shoiab arrived in Omaha, Nebraska, and was met by Merry Ellen Turner and Tom Gouttierre. They took Shoiab and hosted him for one year as he prepped for admission to West Point. West Point had indicated Shoiab needed to work on English and Math skills, then reapply the following year.

Below is the email I sent to Merry Ellen the day Shoiab departed Kabul. Please note, I tried to inflict a bit of humor where I could, so don't believe everything you read.

Merry Ellen,

Well, I have just sent the future West Point Cadet toward the United States or I have lost a kid forever. The movie "Terminal" with Tom Hanks is running rapidly through my brain. Here is why.

With the assistance of Derek Hodgson, bless his heart, we

got a ticket for Shoiab (aka. Scooter) from Kabul to Dubai with an individual meeting Shoiab at the airport in Dubai to give him a ticket to the United States.

Sounds great right! It was, however, Inshallah.

Here is what has happened:

Shoiab is supposed to leave on an American Flight at 1:40 a.m. on 30 September from Dubai. I was told by my people here just wait until the day he is leaving before you get him a ticket. For some reason I chose to go by the airport early this morning to see if there were any problems in getting a ticket. We did not want to fly Areania (sp) airlines (called Inshallah Airlines) because of their canceling of flights all the time, so I went with KAM airlines. KAM flies Wednesday, Saturdays, and Sundays. Areania flies Tuesdays, Thursdays, and Fridays all to Dubai.

I could not get the KAM office to answer or open its doors so I went to the check-in counter and under the KAM sign, they said they didn't work for KAM.

(I'm starting to get a little nervous) Not because of the ticket issue but I left Ray Winkel in the SUV with the windows rolled up and a big smile on his face as he was trying to load his 9mm. I should have cracked the windows.

I am about to scratch the possibility of getting a ticket today and just waiting until tomorrow when Masoom, our interpreter, who was with us, encouraged me to check at the KAM ticket office where we got Shoiab's ticket to go to Pakistan (Where he was arrested).

I went into the KAM office and the agent said that KAM airlines has been grounded and will not be flying for a month. This was 8:30 this morning. The Areania flight was to take off at 9:00. At this time I am about to get real strange. The agent said don't worry that flight never leaves on time and said he would call the airport. What have I got to lose? What I didn't know was that he just didn't call the airport, he called the control tower to find out when the flight would be departing and they said the 9:00 flight could leave at 10:30.

I then try to buy a ticket and he said he didn't sell Areania tickets there, but I could go to another location and get it.

We jumped in the car, called Shoiab's brother, told him to get "Scooter" to the airport and we would meet them there. We go through these security sections of town with Masoom helping us get through the barriers and finally make it to a hole in the wall where they are selling tickets, beef, and small children! Strangest place I ever saw.

Anywho, I got a ticket for Scooter and off to the airport we went. When we got back there, we saw Shoiab's father, brother, a General, and someone I didn't know waiting for Shoiab. When I asked where he was, his father said that he was dragging his mother out the door with her on his ankle crying. I think it was a little emotional.

He finally shows up and he and I made it to the check-in counter where we got him on the plane. All this happened between 8:30 and 9:30. So, how was your day?

I got back to his father and found out that Gary and Ray had lost a vehicle and were going to be late with a meeting with our new commander of the military academy so we had to bid the family "Happy Trails" and we took off back to the compound. While en route, we receive information the vehicle had been found and they were at the meeting after all.

Just before Scooter left for Pakistan, I gave him $150.00 just in case he needed it as an emergency. He needed some of it to bribe the police that arrested him so he could get his visa for the U.S.

Therefore, as he left this morning I gave him another $100.00 and told him, "This is in case you get arrested between here and Omaha!" He returned a big smile which relieved some tension in his mission.

At 10:30 I stood out in the middle of the compound and waived at the Areania flight going overhead and saying to myself, "Dude, you better be on that plane!"

For icing on the cake, I have been trying to get in touch with Renji in Dubai and he has yet to return my emails, so he does not know Shoiab is coming today. I try to contact Caroline Chung at the Embassy and she is in the United States. Soooooo...As a last resort I have emailed Dubai Airport and said there is a young man coming through that is going to need some assistance. Please help him find Renji and get him on the flight to the United States.

In summary, the kid is gone, I think. To Dubai, I think. To the United States, I think. Would someone please write to me if you hear or see him?

—Jim "Don't ever want to be a travel agent" Wilhite

IN RIDES THE CALVARY. SMALL GROUP BUT NICE HORSES.

That was just another day in Afghanistan. We started with a significant amount of interviewing by the West Point group months earlier, followed by months of non-activity, to finally scattering around the city to find a kid to send to the United States and not return for at least five years. Had the ticket agent not had a friend in the control tower, this may not have ever happened, and Shoiab may not have had the chance for a top grade education. Now it was back to our original mission.

At the same time, I was starting to gain support for the mission from strangers and even some Team Has Been Members. The strangers were made up of people that had been assigned to work at the compound and had been double slotted with another individual. A little professional overkill if you ask me.

These individuals had nothing to do and heard about the academy and its mission. Individuals started showing up at my door asking if they could work for me, because this definitely sounded like a great job with a lot of internal satisfaction.

Most commanders were eager to pass along these soldiers to me so they could have something constructive to do. Eventually, I ended up with about a ten member ad hoc team. While it was a temporary fix, it worked well for us.

I also got word from Lieutenant Colonel Bushy, the personnel officer for Kabul Compound, about two personnel that would be joining me the first part of November and would be there for about six months. A Lieutenant Colonel Tim Porter and a Major Doug Hayes would become part of the team to build the academy. I did not know either one of these individuals. They were not West Point personnel, but I could now begin to think that we were actually being recognized. These two individuals would be arriving shortly before Colonel Winkel and Krahn departed.

If we did not have students then it would not be necessary to have faculty, so Colonel Krahn and I began working with a LTC Clint Dawson (Original Team Has Been Member) and his Recruiting Assistance Team (RAT) to get the word out to potential students and develop a plan to market, evaluate/assess, and select our students.

Lieutenant Colonel Dawson and his teams bent over backward to help us in any way possible to develop viable training and communication tools to help with ramping up the recruiters in the various provinces. They traveled all over Afghanistan in an aged Russian Hind Helicopter. We basically had an open seat whenever we wanted to go and meet with the various governors of each province. It was a great experience and excellent opportunity to share the dream of the NMAA with the Governors throughout Afghanistan. Lieutenant Colonel Dawson even had some special flyers made up for distribution.

A major coordination effort was constructed to bring the recruiters from all over Afghanistan to Kabul to the recruiting headquarters for meetings and training. Lieutenant Colonel Dawson provided Colonel Krahn and me the opportunity to conduct training with the various recruiters to tell them exactly what we were looking for. I don't believe I had ever seen such enthusiasm with a bunch of men. They were very excited about the challenge ahead of them. Not only were they recruiting for the Afghanistan National Army (ANA), but now they were going to be responsible for identifying the smartest and brightest high school students in their country and assist in helping develop the next university.

As we were explaining the process and what we needed the

recruiters to do, they got more and more animated. We had approximately two thousand brochures for them to distribute. They were promising us they would have one student for each brochure. That was not exactly what we were after. I told them that many students might be interested, but they needed to be selective with their recommendations. We wanted students that were extremely intelligent, but were also potentially outstanding officers for the future of their country. Basically, I said find someone they would look at as a future leader and that they would follow into battle.

Their enthusiasm did not diminish with the selection process, but some did mention they would be pressured to send certain students that were politically in the circle of leadership. We told them we would do the final selections and not to worry about that. Afterward, Colonel Krahn and I stood outside with the recruiters and the recruiting commander for group pictures and were then returned to Kabul Compound for a debriefing with Colonel Winkel and Dr. Butler. After the debriefing, we began to focus on our selection of academic department heads for the NMAA. That was the next target of opportunity that needed immediate attention.

After much discussion, we came up with our list for the initial selection of faculty and presented the findings to Major General Sharif and Colonel Humdullah. The discussions that followed were very candid and we enjoyed the openness we were starting to get from Major General Sharif. It was obvious this was an extremely intelligent man and that he had taken his assignment very seriously. He had come to the realization that he was given the opportunity to do something that very few soldiers had been able to do: to train and educate students who would have a significant impact in his country. He wanted the best instructors in the academy, regardless of the ethnic background.

As mentioned earlier, not all the Afghans were given the same opportunity to be educated to the level that was needed to be a college professor. As a result, there was not an ethnic balance established when the final list came out. At every step, we had to fight, explain, plead, or do whatever it took to get the approval of the next higher authority to submit a ethnically unbalanced list of instructors. As we told the Minister of Defense Wardak, "Do you want ethnic balance or do you want the best qualified faculty teaching the students?" You pick one or the other, but you can't have both. This was the same information we had been telling our own chain of command.

After presenting our position, we found that we ran into very little opposition with the Afghans. They were tired of war and wanted to rebuild and were willing to bend on the ethnic balance issue for this particular mission. We still had issues with our own American forces. The ethnic balance was still a very sensitive issue, and they could not believe that we could not interview that many people (1,500 applicants screened, over 200 interviews collected, 25 selected) and not get an appropriate balance. It was just not going to happen. There was a significant drop in our educational staff after the leaders were selected. To this day, it still bothers me when supposedly knowledgeable people say we did not consider the ethnic situation in Afghanistan. On the contrary, we did it almost to a fault, but sometimes it just doesn't work out the way we would like it. It is definitely not a perfect world.

We told Major General Sharif and Colonel Hamdullah not to share the recommendations with the candidates, because there may be some that are changed higher up the chain of command. They agreed not to share with anyone and understood the gravity of the situation if they did. However, some were either told by another source or talked themselves into believing they either had or had not been selected.

Because of the leak of information or the perceptions from those interviewed, a situation developed which almost reached crisis level within the ranks of the officers. These interviews had a direct correlation with the careers of these individuals. While many had a limited education, they still believed they had a calling to teach. Only twelve and one half percent (twenty-five) were selected, which left the remaining eighty-seven and one half percent unemployed and upset.

Today as I reflect on that particular component of our mission, I realize just how sensitive that situation was. This was a survival situation with many of these officers. To not be hired as a teacher at the academy might have appeared as being a failure in the eyes of MoD. The options were to go back to a line unit in the Afghan National Army, retire, or be fired.

So now we have an individual, out of a job and with no money coming in for their family. The end result is we have the potential for another person to join the opposing forces. People like that are prime candidates for such an opportunity. It's a simple matter called survival.

Hiring of qualified faculty would be one of the toughest decisions we had to make and handling it as professionally as we could was extremely important. We tried to make sure that those not hired would be able to remain with the military in some fashion. I would like to think we were successful in that particular endeavor.

In the final approval stage, we did not get one hundred percent of our selections approved, but we did get most accepted, which allowed us to start training and preparing for the incoming group of potential cadets that would have to be assessed. It was going to be extremely important that everyone, and I mean everyone, would have to pitch in to make this dog hunt. We now had a basic foundation for the academy and people around OMC-A were beginning to ask questions. "What is this thing you are doing, Wilhite? Tell me more, tell me more."

As we were starting to make plans for the assessment format for potential cadets, I received a phone call from Minister Wardak asking me to come to the MoD for an important meeting. As usual, we all dropped what we were doing and headed over to MoD to see what the problem might be. Minister Wardak had received word that the Konkor Exam had been compromised!

The Konkor Exam is taken by Afghan students for entry into their universities. It is equivalent to the SAT exam that is taken by our college bound students in the United States. There are approximately six thousand questions that are in a pool option, and the

Afghans will select around two hundred of these questions for the annual exam. It appeared that someone had gotten the current exam and had sold/distributed them to students. Instead of taking the exam at the site, many students simply took the one they were given and immediately turned in the one they had completed prior to coming to take the exam.

Minister Wardak wanted us to redo the exam to make it more secure. It would have six thousand questions like the original, but needed to be weighted in the different subject areas and able to provide different tests for different sites, while still maintaining the equal testing opportunities for all.

That was an additional task that we initially were not prepared to address, but we had a lot of respect for Minister Wardak and we wanted to help him if possible. This was a major issue, and if we could solve that problem, we would be in a good position if we ever needed to have something done for us.

Colonel Krahn contacted West Point and had a math colleague by the name of Major Isenhour come to Afghanistan for a couple of weeks. Her primary objective was to help with this problem and provide a solution.

It has been said dynamite comes in small packages, and this was no exception. Major Isenhour was a young lady that, while not very tall, stood head and shoulders over anyone that might have considered themselves capable of solving this particular problem. Major Isenhour worked closely with the Minister of Higher Education and their personnel, putting in twelve to fifteen hours a day to create a new format for the exam. Major Isenhour and Colonel Krahn eventually created a Konkor Exam that had the required six thousand questions in all subject areas for Afghan students, in Dari and the Pashto language, that was computer generated in such a manner as to provide a new and different exam in a couple of seconds.

The Afghans would announce the test date and site, and the night before they would plug in the numbers and immediately a two hundred and twenty question exam would appear for printing.

There was no time for students to know exactly what was going to be on the exam.

Minister Wardak did state, "What if someone gets into the test bank and learns all six thousand questions?"

"Hire him! That is one smart person!" We both got a laugh from his comment and my reply. It should be noted that Colonel Krahn took this problem back to West Point, and through email and other options created the solution that is probably in effect five years later.

Another major piece of the puzzle had been completed as Colonel Winkel and Colonel Krahn were about to depart. Dr. Butler would be staying over to work with the next group coming in that would be further developing the training and development of staff. I can't begin to explain how much I appreciated Dr. Butler during this particular time. He was not only an intelligent man who was totally mission-oriented, but he became my personal counselor as I later began questioning myself and what was happening around me.

STUDENT ASSESSMENT
JOYS/CONCERNS

S hortly after the departure of Colonels Krahn and Winkel, Lieutenant Colonel Scott Eagen and Colonel Pat Genung arrived for their portion of the mission. Lieutenant Colonel Eagen was given the responsibility of developing a process for the assessment phase for the academy selection, as well as to develop the foundation for Cadet Basic Training (CBT) for all incoming candidates who would eventually be selected. The final workup on the CBT would be completed by the next team in a month or so. Eagen's primary responsibility was the assessment process we would be using for our final selection of the cadets for the academy.

None of us had a clue as to how many students would show up for the assessment phase. We felt as though we were planning an event and did not know how many people would actually participate. There might be a few, hundreds, or thousands. After all, we were offering job security, a good education, and shelter for a minimum of four years.

We hoped the information was going out correctly to potential candidates. There was already evidence to the contrary. We were going to make a final selection of one hundred candidates for our inaugural class at the NMAA in Kabul. I received a phone call from an individual in the northern part of Afghanistan that had been telling his students that we were actually going to be sending one hundred students to United States Military Academy (USMA) in West Point, New York.

He was quite disappointed and upset to discover that was not the case. I tried to put a positive spin on the opportunities for education in his country, but I don't know how successful I was. I will say that we did get a significant number of potential candidates from his area when we did the initial assessment at Kabul, so I hope he was still pleased with the possibilities.

Lieutenant Colonel Eagen, along with Dr. Butler and I, had to put together the physical assessment phase, as well as an interview process that would allow the students to express themselves orally and on a written essay component. The assessment program would be done on a three-day cycle, and the number of students for whom we had to make arrangements to house and feed remained a mystery.

While we were doing this, Colonel Genung was looking at additional hires in the area of language, specifically, English, to fulfill a need that we thought would be necessary. According to Kabul University administration, English was the number one foreign language taken by students.

It was at this particular time that Major Isenhour arrived to resolve the problem with the Konkor Exam. Major Isenhour worked closely with the Minister of Higher Education and his personnel and had a limited time to accomplish this project. She was only here a couple of weeks, but worked tirelessly with the personnel here and with Colonel Krahn via the internet back at West Point.

Because of our time crunch, we were unable to use Isenhour

and Krahn's new format for the upcoming test dates. This solution would only be good for the following year. It took time to train the examiners as to the process and how to administer this type of exam. We were going to have to rely on the exams that had been compromised for this first year's class.

We got with the Minister of Higher Education and obtained copies of the previous exams to use for the initial year and moved forward for our preparation of upcoming candidates. We still did not have a clue as to how many would show.

Dr. Butler was putting together the physical assessment component of the candidates. He and I traveled to Kabul Military High School and observed physical training of the Afghan students. Initially we thought they would be relatively weak in some of the areas we had selected, but we were pleasantly surprised as to their physical conditioning and skills, such as endurance, pushups, pull-ups, agility, and most importantly, attitude to perform well.

Later, the selected candidates were to surprise us even more when we had a friendly competition between them and a group of hand-picked U.S. soldiers and a group of our NMAA cadets. The only event the U.S. team won was the Tug-o-War. In that event, size as well as strength mattered. In pushups, relays, and other events they won handily, and everyone had a great time in the process.

I was coming up on my two week leave around the middle of November, and was not going to be available to see the initial assessment of the candidates. By this time, I was very involved with the success of the mission and was reluctant to turn over the responsibility to anyone else.

However, Lieutenant Colonel Eagen did a masterful job in making it happen. I compared it to a duck in the water. It looked smooth on the top, but Lieutenant Colonel Eagen was probably paddling like hell underneath. He trained the personnel we had selected for the academy heads and had U.S. military advisors available to help with the assessment. With the exception of a couple of hiccups, they pulled off the first assessment like they had done it for years.

There were a couple of other things that happened during this time that were joys and concerns. One joy was the arrival of my first full-time officer in the ranks. Lieutenant Colonel Tim Porter arrived at the compound and was assigned to my staff of zero full-time personnel. I immediately appointed him as my deputy, and was very excited to see him in-house. Lieutenant Colonel Porter was from TRADOC (Training and Doctrine Command) at Ft. Monroe, Virginia, and was willing to jump into any fire and put it out. Believe me, he jumped into a number of fires that could have been dangerous. He is personally responsible for getting the Afghan faculty paid after four months of non-payment. I am surprised they didn't erect a statue of him at the academy! His attitude, dedication to mission, and encouragement were like gifts from heaven. Lieutenant Colonel Porter stepped in as one of the major players as we were beginning to receive even more recognition.

The concern was with Colonel Genung and me. Colonel Genung did not like the trip over, did not care for her accommodations, did not like the food, and happened to say the wrong thing at the wrong time. It was something like, "We should just cancel this project and scrap the whole thing. The Afghans can't keep a schedule and this mission will not work."

I wasn't really impressed with the booking arrangements for the flights over either. I would have also loved to have better accommodations, and better food would have been nice. One small problem though: We were in a war zone!

The route of the trip involved extensive security measures, and therefore, was quite inconvenient. We actually had some of the best accommodations around. All one had to do was go down range from where we were and see what sleeping arrangements other units had. In comparison, ours was like living in the Hilton.

Food was as good as you could expect. Even better most days. We even got steak and lobster on Friday nights. I haven't had that since I have returned from Afghanistan. The fruits we had were some of the best I have ever eaten, and overall, the cooks tried to make whatever you needed if they had the supplies. They treated us well, but I guess you can't please everyone.

I could deal okay with that complaining though because, in my many years in the military, I have heard more than once, "If a soldier ain't complaining, then you ain't doing your job." But to "Cancel the mission?" At that point I lost it. I had been fighting for the mission for six months, and having been in country less than a week, she told me the mission should be cancelled?

I unloaded my built-up frustrations on her with a few specific choice words. It was not a time for discussion of the future of the academy, nor was it time for discovery learning and teaching. This is what we are. This is what we are about. And I will not let this mission be scuttled by someone who has just arrived in country and is upset because the Afghans miss some deadlines. After I said my piece, I got up, stormed out of the office, and slammed the door behind me. I recall it was very quiet in that office as I departed.

It should be noted that before I became an officer, I had spent twelve years as a noncommissioned officer, rising to the rank of Sergeant First Class. During those twelve years, I spent ten as a Drill Sergeant and had the honor of being selected as my division's Drill Sergeant of the Year twice and competed in a national completion for the nation's top Drill Sergeant. I taught at the Drill Sergeant Academy in Fort Polk, Louisiana, and Fort Leonard Wood, Missouri. I could make a stone cry at the drop of a hat. Well, like a flashback, my drill sergeant mentality appeared out of nowhere, catching everyone off guard. It was not professional, it was not appropriate, and it was not easy to say things like that to another officer. But it felt good at the time, and as I reflect, I would probably do the same thing again.

I then had another problem to deal with. I had to work on an attitude change with two people, Colonel Genung's and mine. To cancel the mission was not an option, and we still needed to work through our differences before either one of us could be effective.

After an hour or so, I came back to the office and sat down at my computer. I was trying to think of what we could do to resolve a very tense situation. It was still very quiet in the office. Colonel Genung's desk was about two desks from mine, but she felt compelled to send me an email.

"We need to talk," was her remark.

"You are correct and I will buy the ice cream. Meet me at the courtyard by the mess hall," was my reply.

We both got up and walked out to the office without saying a word and went to the mess hall, got some ice cream, and began our healing process so we could move forward. I will give Colonel Genung credit that she would still talk to me. She was a better person than I was.

I am sure LTC Porter was wondering what he had fallen into. Dr. Butler visited with me later to settle me down so I could refocus on the mission. At that time, I started to use him as a listening board for my concerns and feelings. I had six months under my belt, was about to go home on leave, knowing I would have to return to a mission that might or might not fail. Plus, I was still not convinced the support was there to make the final decisions necessary to make it happen. Dr. Butler and I started walking at night for about an hour inside the compound and talked about everything we could think of to get my mind off the day's events. Forever, I am appreciative of his advice and being there when I needed to vent my feelings; be it mission or things happening back at home.

My leave time was coming up quickly and I was very excited to be returning to the United States to see my family and friends. I also had an additional objective to accomplish while back in the United States.

I was scheduled to be on leave for two weeks, which included a three-day trip to West Point where I was to brief the personnel there as to the status. The flight home was long and tiring, but equally exciting. Wherever we went, we were greeted with handshakes and well wishes.

One particular incident will always stay with me. I was in Atlanta waiting to board my flight to Tulsa and was visiting with a young Marine. A lady came up to him and offered to change seats and give him her first class seat.

"Madam, I really don't have a good seat. I am sitting in the very back of the plane."

Her reply was, "Marine, you don't understand. My husband is a Marine and he said if I could ever do something for another Marine, then don't hesitate to help one out. Come with me."

With that comment she took his arm and up to the front they went to change seats. I thought, *now that is a first class lady.*

As I took my seat, the flight attendant came up to me and offered free drinks for the duration of the flight. I informed him that while that was very nice, I was in uniform and not allowed to drink. He left and shortly afterwards the captain of the aircraft came to my seat.

"I understand you can't have a drink and I respect that. However, there is a Marine in first class that has an empty seat next to him. Would you like to ride with him back to Tulsa?"

That I did, and we had a great visit and a wonderful reception awaiting us when we arrived in Tulsa. He rejoiced with his family and me with mine. Heck, I think we even hugged people neither one of us knew.

One year later I happened to have his wife in one of my classes. She brought up the arrival to me and what happened. It truly is a small world.

I'M HOME!

My arrival in Tulsa was a fantastic and refreshing feeling that I had not experienced since May of 2004. It was nice to see the reception for incoming service personnel at various stations. While the Tulsa airport did not have a formal celebration, there were still plenty of people there to shake your hand or give you a hug. They may have been waiting on other individuals but they were glad to see any soldier returning safely.

My daughters, Sarah and Laura, were there with signs but Emily was nowhere to be seen. I thought she was just in the crowd somewhere and that I had missed her. I would have thought she might come to the front of the crowd when she saw me though. As I walked out, I hugged both the girls and said, "Where's your mom?"

"She is in Concourse B."

We were in Concourse A. Basically she was in the wrong location on the other side of the airport.

Before I could reply, they informed me that she had been contacted and was on her way over. That minor error on her part ended up being pretty awesome. Everyone got to see us come together as she ran down the walkway to Concourse A and our reuniting. People were applauding, crying and cheering. It was great!

Prior to that time Emily and I had only been separated from each other approximately two weeks in our thirty one years of marriage. Now I was only going to be home for two weeks before I had to return to Afghanistan, so I wanted to make the most out of my time while in country.

We had a whirlwind of hellos followed by another round of goodbyes during my two weeks at home. We visited my mom, sisters and their families for a couple of days. My mom's health was not good and I was very concerned about her dealing with my redeployment. While worried, she still maintained her support and she was more concerned about how I was doing than her own issues. That was a mainstay with her throughout her life. She was always concerned for other people's welfare.

Emily hosted a reception at our house in Tahlequah; a huge gathering was in attendance. Along with many of my friends were senators and the president and vice presidents of our university. Again, the support my family and I were receiving while I was deployed was extremely gratifying.

A common question asked by many was, "What do you need over there?" I had prepared a list for such questions, just in case I was asked and shared our need and concerns for a taste of home while deployed. My family and friends did not let me down. Shortly after my return to Kabul, packages from home started to arrive which were appreciated by all.

TRAVEL TO WEST POINT AND THE ARMY/NAVY GAME

While home on leave, I still had a briefing to make. I needed to go to West Point and brief the senior leadership of our mission. My visit to West Point was very enlightening. I got a tremendous feeling of confidence from the work and commitment West Point had provided for the success of the mission. Lieutenant General William Lennox, Superintendent of the United States Military Academy, rolled out the red carpet and offered whatever assistance I needed to make the mission successful. I got to meet with the personnel that had been over before me, the individuals that had been there while I was the Chief of the Implementation Team, and the future personnel that would be arriving in the next few weeks.

Lieutenant General Lennox, Brigadier General Kaufman, Dean of Education, and Colonel Barney Forsyth, Vice Dean of Education, inspired me so much while there. Their commitment to the mission only reinforced my feelings that we were going to be successful in our endeavors despite some disbelief at OMC-A concerning whether the NMAA would ever become a reality. The naysayers were dwindling as time progressed to the magic hour.

To make the most of family time, I took Emily and the girls with me to West Point. We stayed with Colonel Naessens and his lovely wife, Marie, and they could not have been more gracious hosts. Marie was a significant aid, visiting with Emily and the girls about deployment issues and how to cope. We spent almost every evening discussing such issues. Up to that point, Emily had to learn as she went along; there were a few significant bumps in the road in that process. Fortunately, I married an extremely intelligent woman and she was able to adjust as needed.

On Friday of that week, we watched as the parade began for

movement from West Point to Philadelphia, Pennsylvania, for the annual Army/Navy game. The parade came right by the Naessens house. Orange County Chopper had designed a special motorcycle for the event and the commandant of troops rode it in the parade. Bands played, cars honked their horns with people cheering. What a spectacular event! It was a culmination of all the week's activities leading up to one of the biggest rivals in college football and we got to be a part of it.

We bid adieu to the Naessens and departed West Point shortly after the parade for our journey to Philadelphia. I had gotten four tickets to the game and wanted the girls to experience this great event. I am not sure who was more excited about the game, me or the girls. Either way we were going to have a great time with our Philly Cheese Steak sandwiches, touring Philadelphia and going to the game.

The Army/Navy game was great as always. It would have been better if Army had actually won, but the atmosphere is like no other college event. There are good natured, fun videos by both Army and Navy cadets on the jumbo screen, patriotic themes everywhere, congratulatory comments made by parents of opposing services schools to each other, flybys of the army helicopters and the navy jets and, last but not least, a low flyby from Air Force One!

Yes, Air Force One with President Bush aboard did a low flyby over Financial Field before landing and the crowd went wild. I thought the roar of the crowd would never end. Everyone stopped what they were doing, including the football players to see our Commander in Chief salute the service schools.

President Bush sat on one side with the Commander of the Midshipmen; at half time he crossed the field and met with Lieutenant General Lennox to join him on the Army side of the field. The girls loved all the pomp and circumstance that was on display throughout the game.

During the fourth quarter of the game it was obvious Army was going to lose, so I turned to Emily and the girls and asked them if they were ready to leave. The bitter cold that day made the score seem that much worse. They indicated they wanted to stay until the end and watch the singing of the services schools as respect for each other. I was thrilled they wanted to do that; to this day they still talk to their friends about attending that game and how much it meant to them.

We returned home and reality sat in as I was preparing to return to Afghanistan. I believe it was more difficult to leave during that time than it was the initial departure. When I first deployed I had no idea what to expect. Now I knew exactly what was going on. I know it was hard on Emily when I first departed, but I can imagine my second departure was almost equally traumatic.

I liken it to losing a loved one, only to have them come back for a brief time then lose them again. I don't want to get morbid about the situation, but I have to honestly say that in my second redeployment, I wondered if I would ever see my family again. That feeling made my trip back to Afghanistan internally emotional. If I ever had stomach problems, they would manifest themselves during this time. I say this to plead with people to respect spouses of deployed soldiers. Unless you have been there and done that, you can never really appreciate what they are going through.

RETURNING TO KABUL

Getting back to Kabul was a little more difficult than getting to the U.S. Because of aircraft issues, I was three days late getting back on mission than initially planned. I promise it had nothing to do with the three days of Temporary Duty (TDY) that I had requested. It was just the nature of the beast. I did not complain about the delay. In fact, I kind of enjoyed it.

Upon my return to Kabul, I got to meet with a new group of personnel who had been preparing for deployment. Lieutenant Colonel Jack Piccuto, Lieutenant Colonel Mike Phillips, Major Brent Novak, Lieutenant Colonel Ray Nelson, Lieutenant Colonel Vern Davis, Lieutenant Colonel Buck Buchanan, Colonel

Gene Ressler, and Colonel Chris King arrived and probably were not aware at the time, but they were about to witness the capstone of the academy and the opening of the NMAA. This was the largest group from West Point to arrive in one segment. To top it off, I had a second person added to my roster full-time. Major Doug Hayes from Ft. Jackson, South Carolina, was assigned to my staff. It appeared someone in personnel was thinking, "Damn, this thing might happen. We better get Wilhite some help." Maybe that is not what they were thinking, but I didn't care; it was great to see the bodies. Major Hayes was a personnel officer who was also a Ranger. What has that got to do with anything? Easy: he could and would do anything. I give him credit for being one of the most influential and persistent officers to reach the final rung in the ladder of success as related to the opening of the academy. It could not have been done without all the people that were involved in the program, but Major Hayes performed in such a manner that I truly believe the academy would not have ever become a reality had he not been assigned to our group. All of these additions were truly additional gifts from heaven.

CADET BASIC TRAINING, FACULTY DEVELOPMENT, AND "THE SIGN"

We were now starting to get nervous. It was close to Christmas and the cadets would be arriving around the first of February. We had to get the Program of Instruction (POI) written for cadet basic training, and it had to be done so that it would accommodate the Afghan culture and training doctrine. Lieutenant Colonel Davis and Nelson took responsibility along with Major Novak to insure we had an acceptable program to train the cadets. We had one minor problem though. Who was going to train these kids? When I departed for leave, Lieutenant Colonel Porter was working with Training and Doctrine Command (TRADOC) out of Ft. Monroe, Virginia, to have a group of noncommissioned officers come to Afghanistan and take responsibility for Cadet Basic Training (CBT) that would be conducted prior to the beginning of course work at the academy for our new incoming students.

Initially it looked very promising; however, when I returned, I was informed the request for trainers from the U.S. had been denied. Someone in the chain of command thought it ridiculous that I would even consider asking for such personnel. I had about twenty drill sergeants from my former battalion who were wanting to volunteer to come over and work with me in putting this academy together, but they were told they could not do that because the reserve unit they were with needed them more. A footnote to that however, is that by the time I had returned home, most of them had been deployed to Iraq.

Colonel King, Lieutenant Colonel Porter, and I went to Major General Sharif to discuss solutions to this problem. Also in attendance was Colonel Tekbas, the Turkish Liaison. As we identified our needs, Colonel Tekbas stepped forward and volunteered soldiers from his country to do all the training. While I was thrilled about the possibilities, Major General Sharif was less than enthusiastic. Sharif knew all too well the training doctrine of the Turks, and really didn't want anything to do with it. However, we didn't have much choice, so we told Colonel Tekbas to follow through and let us know what he could do with the training personnel.

The following day we had to brief the Major General Weston. When I told him about the training problem and the Turkish solution, he became upset and said that would not be an option. Like Sharif, Weston also knew the training policy of the Turks and it was not a process that we could accept for the academy. He started assigning personnel to work with me to insure a group of soldiers (trainers) would get here as soon as possible.

All of a sudden I had almost too many people trying to help. We were about five or six weeks away from the academy opening its doors when about a dozen soldiers, handpicked by Major General Weston and Colonel Baker, Chief, Defense Operation Sector (DOS), began trying to put their two cents worth in to get this plan rolling. To quote Colonel Baker, "Now we are interested!"

My reply was, "It's about time!" As I reflect on the moment, it should have upset me that they waited so long. However, that is how things were operating in this country. I didn't have time to get upset, besides, I needed the help.

Meanwhile, Colonel Chris King was working diligently on the curriculum. Major Brent Novak was developing a training format for a "train the trainer" process, when and if we had personnel to do the training. Lieutenant Colonel Tim Porter was working the pay issue with the Afghans. Lieutenant Colonel Buck Buchanan was working logistics, while at the same time preparing to teach rugby to the cadets. Lieutenant Colonel Jack Piccuto and Lieutenant Colonel Mike Phillips were conducting faculty training in mathematics for both the Afghans and Turkish Instructors who had started to arrive. Colonel Gene Ressler was designing, developing, and establishing a computer program/facility, training Shakeb, our Afghan internet specialist, as well as getting a Web site established for the academy. Lieutenant Colonel Ray Nelson was developing and coordinating the training schedule for a completed Cadet Basic Training program that would meet the needs of the troops. Lieutenant Colonel Vernon Davis was attacking range logistics and equipment issues. Major Doug Hayes was working furniture equipment and classroom logistics, and I was attempting to get the buildings completed before the first cadets arrived.

I was also trying to get Colonel Tekbas to understand that we now had the personnel we needed and that we wouldn't need the Turkish trainers after all. I thought he understood, but somewhere there was a miscommunication in the statement, "We have our personnel for CBT training. We do not need the Turkish trainers."

To this day I don't have a clue as to what part of that statement he did not understand.

I must have been talking to a stone wall, because they showed up to conduct the training anyhow. The problem is they showed up about four days before graduation from Cadet Basic Training and were upset that we started without them. With all the events starting to come together, and at times seeming to start to fall apart, Lieutenant Colonel Nelson compared me to a person juggling chain saws. Maybe that was not a bad comparison.

About three weeks before Cadet Basic Training began, Captain Eric Creviston and First Sergeants Rodney Spade, Steven Ridings, Todd Brown, Anthony Hall, and Paul Young arrived, courtesy of the Indiana National Guard at Task Force Phoenix. They were excited to be a part of the training program. We brought them up to speed as to what was needed and they charged into the mission more than one hundred percent. Their work ethic was outstanding as they prepared training for the incoming cadets. About the same time, the Afghan National Army provided approximately sixteen soldiers to conduct training; the Indiana group started training them as to how to conduct "Western Style" training.

We wanted the cadets to receive an understanding of the military concept in the Afghan National Army as well as establishing leadership opportunities for the cadets. Like West Point, we wanted the National Military Academy of Afghanistan to be about leadership.

We also wanted to eliminate the physical abuse that sometimes comes in the training that Afghans receive. While it was done in the old Afghan Army, we had been trying to assist in eliminating that option in the new Afghanistan National Army (ANA).

I was informed the Turkish Army also utilizes physical abuse of their soldiers. While I can't speak to that personally, we did not want that as an option. I did hear some pretty rough stories from enough Turkish soldiers to validate my concerns though.

A paradigm shift we had to make was allowing the noncommissioned officers (NCOs) to conduct training and the officers to supervise the work being done. The NCO in charge of training falls in line with the western style of training. However, making that change generated a few problems, but I had to give the Afghans credit. They wanted to learn as much as possible and were like sponges to our type of training, both in the military and educational arenas. I often thought about my students here in the U.S. and wished they were as motivated to learn as my Afghan soldiers and students. We really are spoiled in what advantages we have. We are so used to having everything that we take what we do have for granted.

What we take for granted was again brought to my attention as I was conducting a training program with the Afghan faculty. A few years ago I heard a great story from a gentleman by the name of Dr. Miles McCall from Stephen F. Austin University in Nacogdoches, Texas. He compared teaching to fishing. His comments related to someone having the best equipment, lures, boat, etc., but if they didn't know how to present it, the fish wouldn't take the bait. You can have the worst of everything, but if you know how to present it, the fish will take the bait. Students are the same way. If you know how to present with what you have, the students will take the concept you want them to take and run with it. Fishing is not easy. If it was it would be called "Catching."

Teaching is not easy either. If it appears easy, then the teacher has done a significant amount of preparation to present it appropriately to the students. When done correctly, the students will take the bait or concept you are trying to teach.

I loved that story and thought it would be a great time to share that with my new instructors from Afghanistan. I was doing what I thought was my best presentation and in the process of my explanation, I asked the question, "How many of you have been fishing before, either as a child or an adult?" As Dr. Sardar translated the question, I got the strangest look from the faculty and no hands were raised. There was a moment of uneasy silence.

I turned to Dr. Sardar and asked him what was translated and he indicated exactly what I had said. As I turned back to the instructors, Brigadier General Ekbal raised his hand. In broken English he said, "Baba, we have been in a drought for seven years and in war for twenty-five years. We have no lakes, no rivers, no fish." Talk about not knowing your audience, I had to shift gears very quickly. That story did not work.

Later in the same presentation, I thought I knew the answer, but I was not prepared for how it was given to me. I figured they had very little computer training, but thought I would ask any way.

"How many of you have had computer training?"

Again I received silence with the exception of Brigadier General Ekbal. "Baba, it is like water, we have no electricity, with the exception of approximately one hour per day. We have not had any computer training."

I was a bit more prepared for that one. I responded, "That won't be the case before I leave. You will have electricity and computer training. You will also be trained on how to utilize it in the classroom." That was one of the many successes we had with the NMAA. Because of the efforts of Colonel Ressler and the training of Lieutenant Colonels Piccuto and Phillips, as well as assistance from the Turkish faculty, every faculty member was trained and developing their own power point presentations for class. I was called to the classroom many times to see their work, and I don't know who was more excited to see such success, me or them.

It is said, "Success builds on success," and that was never more evident than the Afghan officers who were working, learning, and performing with their new found tools, computers, and electricity!

THE BABY IS BORN

In conjunction with the class training was the preparation for the arrival of students. February 5, 2005 was getting close, and we had to look at the format we wanted to use for an efficient in-processing procedure. It had to be seamless and professionally done. We knew we would be looked at closely by MoD personnel, and the impression we made would be paramount.

Everyone had to be involved. It would be a collective effort of all personnel. We had convinced the Afghan faculty they were the best who would be teaching the best to be the best and they had to work above and beyond their normal jobs for this to happen. We only had twenty-five personnel to conduct the in-processing. The NCOs and Tactical Officers were still in training, so the entire faculty and staff had to get the students checked-in, bedded down, fed, clothed, medically examined, and oriented, all of which lasted approximately three days. Everyone had a job that did not normally fit his initial job description, but all pitched in, including Major General Sharif, to make it happen. As an example of everyone needing to work, I wanted to use another "Oklahoma Proverb."

"Everyone must work together, even with the simplest of tools, to build a mighty building." Is that an Oklahoma Proverb? Not exactly, but I was on a roll and needed to use something that would get their attention.

To show what I was talking about, I handed Major General Sharif a small knife and I pulled out a small knife. I asked him, "Would you cut down the largest tree on these grounds with the smallest knife to have a successful academy?" He smiled and nodded that he would. Even if it was not an actual proverb, the faculty got the idea and everyone pitched in to make the in-processing run as smoothly as possible.

The faculty also contributed more than just the in-processing. They started grabbing shovels and rakes and started cleaning up around the academy grounds. I was quite proud of myself, but more proud of the faculty and staff who really wanted this experience to be successful.

It was hard to have an academy without a name in front of it. The air academy sign was still hanging, even though we had earlier evicted them from the facility. For three months I had one heck of a time getting the sign down and a more appropriate one in place.

We had one made, but it was in hiding for just the right time. That time came when the cadets showed up at the front gate.

On February 5, 2005, we opened our doors for the cadets to arrive. We had issued one hundred and twenty invitations to the first group of applicants. We had over three hundred and fifty apply for the first class. The one hundred and twenty were all ethnically balanced by the break down of the national information we had. The only problem was that not all provinces were represented. But then again, not all provinces submitted applications.

One of the first cadets who arrived was a young man who had scored the highest in the nation on the Konkoor Exam. He spoke five languages and was a wonderful addition and set a very high standard for the academy.

The baby was officially born on 5 February 2005! The NMAA was now in operation and open for business.

One of the visitors that day was MoD for Education Fawzi. As I saw him coming, I placed my right hand across my chest. As he got closer, I extended my hand to shake his. Instead, he threw his arms around me and gave me one of those Afghan hugs and said, "Put up the sign. I will issue the order. No one will argue."

I cannot describe how important that comment was to me. In Afghanistan, signs mean everything, and the changing of the sign was a major step in establishing ownership of not only the NMAA, but also of the grounds where we would be in operation.

I smiled, placed both my palms across my chest and said, "Tashakur" (thank you) and quickly excused myself. Along with Major General Sharif and Dr. Sardar, I went to retrieve our sign. We took it to the front gate and I began trying to climb the wall and take down the Air University sign. The Afghan personnel did not want me to climb the wall, because they were afraid I would fall and hurt myself. They asked me to step down and they would put it up. There was no way I was going to let someone else do that, so I just told them to catch me if I fell. I really think they would have done it too. They all got together and helped me climb the wall and stood there laughing, clapping, and singing while I dismantled the first sign and put up the NMAA sign. As I completed putting up the sign, I raised my hands in victory and someone took my picture. That picture ended up on the front page of "The Pointer View," which was the West Point Newspaper and became know as, "The Great Sign Caper!"

Regardless of what it was called, we now had a more solid foundation from which to work. I thought that if we didn't have some type of symbol, the academy could go away with a simple stroke of a pen. Remember, we were born that day and the survival rate of newborn babies in that country is not as good as it should be. We still needed to crawl and walk before we could run.

THE GRAND OPENING DEBATE

MoD wanted to have its grand opening on February 5, 2005, but I insisted that we wait until Cadet Basic Training was completed. I had a method to my madness, and fortunately MoD Wardak and Education Minister Fawzi liked my plan.

The plan and rationale was fairly simple. If we had a grand opening the day they arrived, the following problems would be involved.

- They would not all be arriving at the same time.

- The weather could be bad, (It was snowing pretty badly on February 5)

- They would not have uniforms.

- They would not know how to march.

- The facilities would not be completed.

The bottom line was pretty simple: If you want this to be the "Crown Jewel," then it must look like a crown jewel.

Solution: If we have the Grand Opening on March 22, 2005,

all the problems mentioned above would be non factors. T h e y agreed and I got an additional seven weeks before I had to showcase the "Crown Jewel of Afghanistan."

Of the 120 cadets we had initially sent invitations to, approximately one hundred and five arrived the first day. An additional ten or so arrived a few days later because of the bad weather. However, one individual did not arrive until the fourth week of Cadet Basic Training. Major General Sharif would not accept him at the academy because he was so late. He did relent, though, and allowed the young man to visit with me before he made his final decision. As mentioned earlier, Sharif and I had a great relationship and he trusted my judgment on many issues.

The young man had started from the Hindu Kush mountain area about twenty kilometers from the Chinese border. He began his trip about three weeks before the initial opening of school. Early in his trip, he had a car wreck so he abandoned his car and continued on foot. He was then robbed while en route and, for the past seven weeks or so, he was begging for food/money, hitchhiking, and wearing the same clothes every day. For him to return home would have been a disgrace for him as well as for his family. The repercussions of such a failed attempt were unthinkable. I could not, in good conscious, send him home.

I stuck out my hand and said, "Son, welcome to the National Military Academy of Afghanistan!" We took him to the clothing issue point, got him outfitted, and then assigned him a room and had him take a shower. He was so excited when he returned from the clothing issue site; he now had something else to wear. I suggested he burn the clothes he had, which he gladly did. He did not even complain the next morning about having a fifteen kilometer hike. He was a real trooper and basically mirrored the attitude of all the NMAA cadets. They were there for an education and to serve their country in the military; they were there to make a better life for themselves and their families.

JUGGLING CHAIN SAWS

Cadet Basic Training went very well with Lieutenant Colonel Davis and Buchanan, and others successfully staying ahead of the power curve and providing assistance to Captain Creviston and his NCOs. It was extremely important that transportation and ranges were coordinated, and Lieutenant Colonel Davis suffered some frustrations in making this happen. The ranges were about twenty miles from the academy and issues like time for pickup and delivery both to and from the ranges were extremely important. Also, fuel requirements and consistency of the drivers were factors that had to be addressed.

Lieutenant Colonel Davis had that West Point initiative though, and was like a pit bull staying after whatever tasks that needed to be accomplished, and succeeding at a high level of effectiveness. I will have to admit, it was sometimes interesting to listen to him, in his corner of the office, sigh really big and roll his eyes into the back of his head.

Colonel King continued to write and rewrite the curriculum, schedules, and degree plans for our majors, as well as a student handbook that was to be carried and learned by each cadet. Colonel King spent a significant amount of time at the Ministry of Higher Education getting appropriate information for the material he was putting together.

Lieutenant Colonel Buchanan got an additional task of preparing to coordinate the arrival of Brigadier General Daniel Kaufman, the Dean of Education at West Point, along with his staff and special VIP, Vincent Viola, a West Point graduate and an owner of the New Jersey Nets Professional Basketball Team.

Protocol dictates special arrangements be made for general officers and their staffs. Lieutenant Colonel Buchanan was in contact with both the West Point and Kabul Compound protocol offices on a daily basis, and what sometimes seemed an hourly basis, making sure every event was seamless. He did his work well! All VIP personnel arrived a day or two early, tired but excited about the grand opening scheduled for March 22, 2005.

GRAND OPENING OF THE NATIONAL MILITARY ACADEMY OF AFGHANISTAN

(MISSION COMPLETE)

Image is everything in Afghanistan and the opening of the NMAA was no different. Major Doug Hays was placed in charge of bidding the monies that we had received from MoD to buy furniture and equipment for the academy. The problem was the process that is utilized at the Ministry of Finance. Major Hays had to identify every piece of equipment, including test tubes, staplers, desks, furniture, and faculty equipment. Absolutely everything that was needed to start the academy had to be identified.

After that list was compiled, it had to be taken to the Ministry of Finance. They advertised the equipment and in came the vendors. Major Hays, his translator, Rafee, and whoever I was upset with on my staff had to go down to MoD Finance and sit through the bidding process. That was probably the best discipline format I could have used, for attending the bidding process was truly a punishment simply because of the format.

The vendors were required to bring cash money and Major Hays would come back in the afternoon shaking his head and absolutely worn out. The Afghans would argue with each other, with Major Hays, with anyone that would listen. They also made threats to Hays and others. I don't think anyone would have argued with Major Hays if he requested to step back and say to hell with the whole bidding process.

"Test tubes, how much for test tubes?" They would go around the room bidding until a final bid was approved. "Staplers, how much ..." and they would repeat the process. Then, of course, we needed staples and the circus would start again. This took at least two weeks to get the initial process done. I say initial because once that was completed, it was published in the Afghan paper with the low bids and additional vendors were allowed to come to MoD Finance and bid again. Therefore the entire process started over.

While this was happening, my wife, children, and students from Northeastern State University were shipping school supplies to our site to start the academy, just in case we didn't have material ready when classes actually began.

As the bidding process was finally completed, Major Hays started receiving equipment about ten days before the grand opening. Now we really had to go to work, because painting still needed to be completed.

As the Grand Opening got closer, our work continued to build and tensions got higher. Major General Weston departed shortly before the grand opening, so he did not get to see the ceremonies. To be honest, until the last couple of months, I really don't think MG Weston thought the NMAA would become a reality. A lot of people under him made comments that gave me that impression. This is not to take away from Major General Weston. He was an extremely focused individual on the mission of Afghanistan and as he said, this was a "nice to do" component of the mission. I can honestly understand his feelings, but fortunately, I took it a little more personal than that.

Shovels had been issued to the faculty. Major General Sharif and I had our small knives out, symbolic of the idea that we would do what it takes to make mission complete. Contractors were working diligently to have classrooms ready, the West Point personnel were working their magic, and the Crown Jewel was getting polished and about to be unveiled.

I have to admit that the last few weeks I had doubts as to whether we would actually accomplish this mission; not because of our efforts, but because time was getting short. To use an old skydiving term, we were starting to get "ground rush." While you are high in the air you have a floating sensation. Events, deadlines and last minute changes were happening so fast I thought I was in free fall without a parachute. We were getting ground rush and the results could be tragic.

The cadets had arrived and were conducting Cadet Basic Training and soon would be ready for the first day of class. We had some pretty high ranking individuals that were coming out for the big event and it would not be good form to have a bad showing of the grand opening. I had also convinced MoD not to have the grand opening the day students arrived. I also assured them of great weather and impressive new young soldiers. It would be something of which they would be proud.

The Army engineers were wandering around the academy with checklists that needed to be met before they were signed off and handed over to the Afghans. While I understand their concern, I couldn't help but feel they might throw something in the mix that would destroy everything we had worked toward. Was I starting to get paranoid? Yes, but at this time paranoia was about all I could hang my hat on. Then more prayers were answered.

TRAINERS FROM THE U.S. ARRIVE

During the training period, Lieutenant Colonel Paul Lalley arrived with a crack group of NCOs who had experience with training cadets at the United States Military Academy at West Point. They knew something about Cadet Basic Training; in fact, they knew everything about Cadet Basic Training. The NCOs did not need to be trained very much because of their knowledge, so the handoff from Captain Creviston's team was basically seamless.

Colonel Tekbas was still trying to get his officers and NCOs into the mix and, about a week before Cadet Basic Training was completed, they showed up ready to train the cadets. Cadet Basic Training was about six weeks long and four weeks had already passed. With the arrival of Lieutenant Colonel Lalley and his men, the Turkish personnel were not needed. To say they were upset is an understatement. They were not upset with us, but with Colonel Tekbas, because they had only five days notice before coming to Afghanistan and had arrived with nothing to do. The initial discussion for Turkish troops had been conducted almost two months before and within seventy-two hours of that first discussion, Colonel Tekbas was told they were not needed. I don't know why they were only given five days notice. I don't even know why they came.

To add insult to injury, Colonel Tekbas was trying to get the Turkish Band to perform at the grand opening, and the MoD representatives did not want that to happen. Colonel Tekbas had harassed Lieutenant General Krimee at home and at work about the Turkish band as well. MoD wanted the U.S. National Anthem played along with the Afghan National Anthem. We had informed MoD that this was an "Afghan thing" and only the Afghan National Anthem should be played. Basically, all the attention was to be directed to the Afghans. However, the Turkish issue further complicated things. Chief of Staff Lieutenant General Krimee stated, "He (meaning Colonel Tekbas) is making me extremely tired. I think we should consider option seven!"

That comment was made the morning of the grand opening and it really got my attention. In their country, they use English words that have a slightly different meaning, but the point certainly gets across. Comments like, "I'm losing my personality" mean I am losing my mind. "You are making me tired," is translated to, "You are upsetting me." "You are making me extremely tired," is pretty much interpreted as, "You are making me extremely angry!" Option seven was something I came up with as a joke, but it was taken seriously.

Earlier in the building process, Colonel Tekbas was starting to make the entire MoD and OMC-A chain of command "extremely tired." The higher-ups in both chains were getting so involved in the issues Tekbas had created that our work at the academy was grinding to a halt. Because of that situation, I drafted a seven plan option.

Of the seven options, two and five were the most viable. I did want to give Colonel Tekbas some options to choose, and I could have lived with any of the initial six. It's just option two and five were the best. Those were the two I was going to push and I thought I could have been successful in convincing Tekbas to consider one of those two options. After all, according to him, I was his best friend. (The man must have been abused as a child!) Option seven was initially submitted as a joke, but the crowd received it a bit differently than how I meant it.

I presented the options to MoD and OMC-A and emphasized the importance of options two and five. I then indicated if he didn't commit to option two or five, we can add then together and have an option seven. "What is an option seven?" asked the Afghans.

"We can kill him!" I said. There was a mixed reaction, none of which were humorous reactions. OMC-A did not see any humor in that, and MoD took it very seriously.

I said I was just kidding and was trying to break the tension with everyone. Option seven should not be considered. While the Afghans discarded "Option Seven," they never forgot and brought that to my attention more than once. It would always make me a little nervous; I am glad they never actually executed that option. As I reflect on their timing, I think they were just looking for a reaction from me when they discussed it, because we always ended up laughing. Humor gets strange in a war zone. In the end, Colonel Tekbas chose one of the two options I was emphasizing and we never had to follow through with anything else.

THE BABY IS CRAWLING

It was now March 22, 2005 and the Grand Opening was just a few hours away. The second coat of paint had just been placed on the grandstand and we were all hoping and praying it would be dry before the ceremonies got started. We had individuals out with towels and blankets fanning the grandstand trying to get the paint dry. The day was beautiful, just as I had promised a couple of months before. Never mind that it rained buckets the day before. We were going to have a beautiful day for a grand opening and a parade. Everyone was scrambling, trying to make the facility look just right. The cadets had completed Cadet Basic Training and were starting to get dressed for the formal ceremony. Colonel Tekbas was nowhere in sight, but, for some reason, I had this uneasy feeling.

Lieutenant General Krimee was still wanting to lean toward "Option Seven," and I used all my diplomacy to convince him that to do that would take away from this great day we were about to have. I reminded him of the initial concerns we had and what great accomplishments everyone had shared in to make this a special day. On February 5, the students did not know how to march, they did not have a military bearing, the weather was bad, the buildings were not completed, the grounds and grandstand were in terrible shape, and the furniture had not arrived, just to name a few of the concerns.

On March 22, 2005, the cadets were marching so well that they had been selected as the honor group for the Independence Day cerebration held later in April. That event is a national holiday for Afghans to celebrate when the Russians left Afghanistan. They had extremely high military bearing, the weather was beautiful, even though it rained like crazy the day before, and enough buildings were complete that the students and faculty had classrooms and offices. The grandstand and grounds were in much better shape (paint almost dry), the dining facility was complete, and good Afghan food was aplenty. It couldn't have been a more perfect day and I was about to pop my buttons on my uniform because I was so proud of everyone's work. And then . . .

Around the corner comes the Turkish band. I was in shock. Lieutenant General Krimee's eyes glared like a man possessed. All I could see in his eyes was "Option Seven." Turkish television cameras were being set up. Colonel Tekbas came out and rearranged the seating assignments and put himself and his commander on the front row. He was talking to anyone that would listen about all the work he had done with very little assistance from any other allied force in developing the NMAA, which he was referring to as "His Baby."

I thought about all this hard work and effort going right down the drain because of this man. At this time I was "extremely tired" of his actions, but I still had to focus on the mission at hand. It was imperative that we move forward with a front that appeared to be in total control. A concern I had was that the grand opening would implode on itself. The level of tension was so high that I would swear the temperature got about twenty degrees higher in about ten seconds. I had gone from feeling excited about the ceremony beginning to start, to becoming nauseous. If I was to ever get an ulcer, this would be the time and place. Krimee was starting to move toward Tekbas.

I pulled Lieutenant General Krimee to one side and indicated how important it was to focus on the grand opening with all the publicity that would be favorable for his country. I pointed to the television cameras, the press corps, and dignitaries. We could deal with Colonel Tekbas later. I felt fortunate that my relationship with such a distinguished man was to a point that he yielded to my suggestion and did nothing at that time. It was only a matter of time, though, for Colonel Tekbas.

THE BABY'S FIRST STEPS

The dignitaries that came to the grand opening were from all our allied forces. I was certainly glad to see our new OMC-A Chief, Major General John Brennan, in attendance. Since Major General Weston had redeployed back to the United States and could not make the event, this was the next best thing. We also had as guest speakers, Major General Mohammad Sharif, NMAA Commander, Abdul Rahim Wardak, Afghanistan Minister of Defense, and Abdul Karim Khalili, Second Vice President of Afghanistan, which bode well for the academy. The following comments of Minister Wardak and Second Vice President Kahalili were taken from the United States Department of Defense Journal. The contributors were Major Rick Peat and LTC Frederick Rice, Public Relation Officers for Kabul Compound. These writings were special to the American Forces Press Services. The articles were available to all military services, but rarely did the U.S. newspapers pick up on the writings, because it was good news.

Minister Wardak: "The role of this academy is vital for the future of Afghanistan, because this academy will produce loyal, professional, and true leaders for Afghanistan's future without any ethnic, language and tribal distinction. These young cadets will be trained in the spirit of national unity and strong military character upon which we can be proud among the respective nations of the world."

Second Vice President Khalili who emphasized the excellent reputation the ANA has built among the people of Afghanistan. "The people of Afghanistan appreciate and strongly support the good work of their integrated national army, which represents the true face of the Afghan nation. Today we are going to open an institute which will train the future commanders and leaders of our proud army and of this hopeful nation.

A part of the ceremony included unveiling the new NMAA flag and the Afghan National colors and flag and having them posted over the grounds for the first time. Also, Brigadier General Daniel Kaufman, Dean of Education at West Point, presented Major General Sharif with a saber from West Point mounted in a nice case for his office. Major General Sharif presented, to Brigadier General Kaufman, a carved wooden plaque of the NMAA shoulder sleeve that had been designed by Colonel Ed Naessens.

Major General Sharif spoke highly of the goals of the academy to teach international standards and national unity for their country. I was proud of my brother as he showed much pride in the second stage of the academy. Remember, the baby was born on February 5, 2005. It was now March 22, 2005 and the baby is about to walk! However, before we walk we had to listen to the Turkish Band.

They performed a nice presentation of their cultural music. When completed, they got an ovation from the crowd. Not a thunderous ovation, but a nice applause. I guess it was good enough that they did their entire show again. When they finished, people basically stared at them in disbelief. I think they were afraid to applaud again for fear another round might ensue, and then gun shots would follow.

They finally marched off into the sunset, or a mine field, or at least somewhere else, and it was now time to have the "Pass in Review" of the new troops. This is where the soldiers, in their best marching skills and military bearing, march past the commander and audience and look very sharp during the ceremony. I was sitting back, watching all of this and honestly feeling quite proud of what had been accomplished, but also knowing that everyone at the ceremony was armed with weapons and live ammunition.

As the cadets prepared to pass in review, Major General Sharif got my attention and motioned for me to join him with the honored guests and stand for the passing of the troops with the Second Vice President and Minister of Defense. It was their show and I was willing to stay in the background, but Sharif insisted I join him. I was truly honored to be a part of the session. I got up and stood proudly by my brother as the troops began marching by.

All of a sudden, I felt two hands grab my shoulder and move me to the right, and a person stepped between me and Major General Sharif. As I looked to my left, I saw Colonel Tekbas standing between me and Sharif. The look on Sharif's face was priceless. I thought to myself,

"Please, no option seven. Please, no option seven."

What in the world is going to happen? Will there be a shoot out in the middle of a ceremony? I looked at Major General Sharif, shrugged my shoulders, and patted my palm to the ground, which meant, "It is okay! We will deal with it later, don't do something stupid." Or it could have also meant, "Please put a dog under my palm so I will have something to pet, because I look pretty stupid patting an invisible dog!" Regardless of what it meant, my brother, General Sharif just smiled and went back to attention for the remainder of the parade.

After the ceremony was completed, photographers took pictures of anything they thought would be of historical significance. I was not fortunate enough to do that because I had a press conference to attend as Chief of the Implementation Team. I only took a couple of pictures and then raced off to a pressroom for questions and comments.

Press corps from all over the world, except the U.S., were at the meeting. I will say Reuters was present, and maybe something was picked up by them, but I never heard anything being played in the U.S. about the academy, and I had friends all over the United States looking for it.

We spent approximately one hour answering questions. It was the first time that much attention had been focused on the academy, and I still couldn't help but be a bit nervous concerning what would be asked or said.

Overall the news conference went well. There was excitement by the Afghans about a new beginning for their country in the area of education. I felt good that I could share in the fortunes that would evolve from this mission. It was one of the best days I had while in the Army. It was a rarity. I actually got to see a mission to the end. That was unusual for this type of war.

As a summary of the day's events, I told the press corps that prior to the ceremony beginning, I went to each cadet and individually shook their hand and wished them good luck. I said that in doing so, I was participating in a significant part in the history of Afghanistan, because I felt that I was shaking the hand of future leaders, future generals, and possibly future Ministers of Defense.

I also mentioned to the press corps a conversation that I had with a young cadet that spoke five languages. I had said to him, "You know we are going to offer the five languages you speak plus two additional languages?"

His reply was, "Yes Baba, I know. I plan on taking those languages also."

I added, "Do you know how valuable you are going to be to this country being able to speak seven languages?"

His answer, "Yes Baba, one day I will be President of Afghanistan."

You know, I think I had just shaken the hand of the future President of Afghanistan. That was immediately followed by a standing ovation from the press corps.

Later we feasted at the dining facility, then retired to Major General Sharif's office. As we were visiting, I said to General Sharif, "Sir, my mission is complete. It's time for me to go home." Sharif, the war-weary soldier, hero of his countrymen, tough as nails individual immediately had tears in his eyes and it was contagious. They welled-up in my eyes also, and we embraced each other knowing that we had been through a lot together the past year, and we were starting to realize one of us was leaving, possibly never to return or to see each other again.

The following day, the West Point group and I joined Major General Sharif as we toured the educational facility and observed the teachings of the faculty. I still could not believe that less than one year earlier we had nothing and now we were moving forward with great progress. We were not there yet, and wouldn't be for about three or four more years, but it was a beginning. My concern was, what type of commitment would be made to sustain and continue to build on this jewel? Once again, a supreme being stepped into my life.

LIEUTENANT GENERAL EIKENBERRY RETURNS

I found out that the new commander for the Afghan mission was Major General (Promotable) Karl Eikenberry, which was fantastic news for us. Eikenberry was the initial OMC-A Chief that got this snowball rolling, so we had that support in our corner and everything was ready for the next phase of the mission.

I had a problem, however, in my redeployment. There was going to be a gap between my coming home and my replacement, Colonel Dean Stroder, coming over. We needed someone to fill the gap. My hero from an earlier deployment, Dr. Larry Butler, stepped to the plate and hit a home run. He volunteered to return to Afghanistan and fill that void until Colonel Stroder arrived. That made the transition much easier, and I felt more comfortable leaving without the fear that everything would fall apart before a replacement arrived. Things happen in that country so fast that the mission being canned would not have been out of the ordinary. We had to fight for every penny we could get.

As I was preparing to redeploy, a going-away ceremony was conducted by the OMC-A personnel. It was not for just me. It was a normal situation that every soldier gets to participate in while over there. They get to say last words and comments before they return home. It is a very special time for those individuals, as well as for those of us that remain when they leave. We have developed lifelong friends during such trying circumstances.

During my time in front of everyone, Major General Brennan indicated that I would be receiving the Bronze Star for my work. The narrative read:

The Bronze Star Medal

To: Colonel James W. Wilhite, Combined Forces Command-Afghanistan

For: Exceptionally meritorious service while serving as the head of the National Military Academy Implementation Team, Defense Operations Sector, Office of Military Cooperations-Afghanistan, Combined Forces Command- Afghanistan, in support of Operation Enduring Freedom. Colonel Wilhite proved himself a man of vision, perseverance and ingenuity as he planned, organized and implemented a four year military academy program which will educate and train the future leaders of the Afghan National Army. As part of this process he coordinated and supervised the staff work of numerous West Point Staff faculty members on academy policy, admission standards and curriculum development, as well as the selection and training of the academy instructors from the local population resulting in the selection of 120 Afghans as the first Corps of Cadets for the academy. His performance of duty in a combat zone reflect great credit upon him, Combined Forces Command-Afghanistan, and the United States Central Command.

David W. Barno, Lieutenant General,
US Army Commanding
R.L. Brownlee, Acting Secretary of the Army

There was your basic ovation and speeches done by people, including myself, after the awards were made. I wanted to make a special comment to one individual while I had my couple of minutes on the stage; to Colonel Laurent Baker, Defense Operation Sector, Chief, a great marine and former football player who worked a group of people from all services as well as any human being could. I used football terminology in my work with him and told him to keep pressing down the field and not to fumble the ball any more than necessary. As I finished my presentation, I pitched to him an NFL football signed by Bill Cowher, head coach of the Pittsburgh Steelers. Their trainer, Chet Furhman, got that for Bake because I felt he was one of the most influential people I met while over there.

MISSION COMPLETE! NOW WHAT?

After that ceremony, I definitely became a short-timer. It is true that your last few days in a combat zone, you get somewhat gun shy. It did cross my mind that I didn't want to do something stupid and become a casualty statistic in this war. I continued doing my work, but handed more and more responsibilities outside the wire to soldiers who were incoming. Lieutenant Colonel Lalley and his team were to stay over, and their work during the transition was of utmost importance.

I made a trip over to MoD to pay my respects to Minister Wardak and Minister Amin, as well as others that I had worked with. I left truly feeling they were thinking they/we were on the right track to get their country back on its feet and moving forward for a better future.

While over there, I saw Colonel Tekbas walking in a garden. I found out he had been banished from the NMAA and was about to be expelled from Afghanistan. He had snuck in to the academy grounds, called a formation, and was lecturing all the cadets on how the academy was his idea and his baby and how he had just about accomplished the entire mission on his own. He was caught by Major General Sharif and was no longer welcomed back at the academy without risk of arrest.

Colonel Tekbas wanted to know how he could get back into the academy again, and I responded, "You're on your own, Scooter." I had waited all year to call him "Scooter." I departed MoD with Colonel Tekbas wondering why I called him a noun! It should be noted that shortly after the grand opening, Tekbas was expelled from Afghanistan and returned to Turkey. I have not written him since returning home, but I often wonder what he is up to. He referred to the NMAA as his baby when he actually was more like a flaw in the jewel that we were building. I do admit that I felt sorry for him because of the tremendous pressure that was placed on his position by his country.

Also, we had an evening ceremony/dinner with Major General Sharif and his staff. When you have ceremonial evenings in Afghanistan, there are always significant gift exchanges. I presented Major General Sharif and his staff with pocket watches that had the NMAA emblem on them, which they appreciated very much. As a group, we also presented Sharif with a significant scrapbook that had been coordinated and put together by Major Hays' wife back in the United States. I will admit that I was envious of his gift. It was one of the finest pieces of work I have ever seen.

Major General Sharif presented to our group a variety of gifts that were extremely nice. A young doctor once told me, "Our country is poor, our people are poor, and our gifts are poor."

I corrected him immediately with the following response, "Your country may be poor and your people may be poor, but your gifts are priceless, because they come from the heart and you just can't put a price on that." I have never met a more gracious group of people.

General Sharif presented me with a beautiful rug, which I proudly display in my entryway at home. The translators gave me an Afghan Flag with their group picture in a flag display box, which I also proudly display in my office. The whole ceremony was very touching and emotional.

It was also during this time that I got a phone call from West Point and found out that the son of Colonel Hamdullah, the Dean of Education for the NMAA, had been selected to attend West Point after having completed a year of prep at the University of Nebraska, Omaha. Colonel Hamdullah and I hugged and shed tears over this selection. It was great for his family and his country.

As the evening was winding down, I received a surprise gift from my own staff. I mentioned earlier that a scrapbook was presented to General Sharif, of which I was envious. It was all in Dari and gorgeous. An exact replica of his scrapbook, in English, was presented to me by my staff. I couldn't believe it. A wonderful representation with a twist of humor for a long year away was truly appreciated. What a night we had.

The following morning, I carefully packed as much "stuff" as I could and started shipping it home. It would take three to four weeks to arrive, but I did not want to carry anything that might slow me down as I was redeploying back to the United States. I ended up sending six large boxes, four of which were footlocker size, back home. I also gave away many items that I thought Dr. Sardar or someone in his family might need, ranging from clothes to Tylenol.

On May 7, 2005, Tahlequah Time (CST), I wrote a letter to Northeastern State University President Larry Williams. I asked that he share the contents with the students at graduation. Many of the education students knew I was in Afghanistan and would be redeploying home soon. I understand it got quite an ovation from the crowd at the football stadium when Dr. Williams read:

> "I know today is a big day for you. Many years of hard work are about to be realized with your graduation from Northeastern State University. I would like for you to know that this day is a big day for me also. As you are sitting in your chairs, I am sitting at a picnic table in Bagram, Afghanistan eating a Whopper from Burger King, a large order of fries, and a large Dr. Pepper, for I am coming home today! I will redeploy back to the U.S. as my mission is complete here and will be back on campus in a couple of weeks."

I GOT BY WITH A LITTLE HELP FROM MY FRIENDS

Initially, getting home was not going to be that easy. We had numerous stops before we actually got to Germany, then had to catch a commercial flight out of Germany to Atlanta. However, with the help from Lieutenant Colonel Mike Phillips; he, along with Lieutenant Colonel Tim Porter and I got a direct flight out of Bagram to Frankfurt. It was long, but it was nice to have that space available, and flying from East to West, we were actually gaining time.

When we arrived in Frankfort, we were immediately placed on a flight to the U.S.; on Mother's Day, May 8, 2005, I was in Atlanta attempting to check-out a car to go to Ft. Benning. This was actually the only problem I had. I did not know that cars were so hard to come by in Atlanta on Mother's Day. I went from venue to venue and they were all sold out.

At one site, a customer service representative had a name of an independent rental car agent that might be able to help me. I made contact with the individual and he did have a couple left, so I snatched one up. Lieutenant Colonel Porter and I loaded in the car and headed to Ft. Benning to do our final out-processing. We sang, laughed, and giggled all the way to Benning.

Along the way to Ft. Benning, I stopped and called my mother to wish her a Happy Mother's Day. She became very emotional when I told her that the best gift I could give her was to return safely to the U.S. and that the mission was complete. I was calling her from Atlanta. My mother had been very ill and told me that she was waiting for me to return before she checked-out. Sadly, she died about sixty days after I returned home, but I did get to spend some quality time with her before her passing.

When I returned to Ft. Benning, I ran into the same type of road blocks that I had prior to deploying. However, they were a bit more receptive to my comments and suggestions. Also, I developed the philosophy that I always told my students who were seniors and felt they were getting the run-a-round before graduating. I told them to have a "Cooperate and Graduate" attitude and it will work out. Now I had to practice what I preached.

I was told that because I came back a couple of weeks early, I needed any o6's signature on my paperwork for approval and not his executive officer. Myself, being an o6, would not count. It had to be a different o6. If I didn't have that signature, then I would have to remain at Ft. Benning until they received it. I heard that was a potential problem and had already put a word in to the executive officer, a major who I thought might be in contact with him. I got on the phone and called Afghanistan and had them fax the information that was needed with the appropriate signatures. I also knew of several "Team Has Been" members that would be returning after me, so we eliminated that problem by getting the appropriate signatures with the appropriate rank before they redeployed to the U.S.

After that issue was resolved, I had to turn in all my equipment that I checked-out before deploying or be held accountable for and pay for everything. I think I could have gotten away with paying for everything except the 9mm I had checked-out. For some reason, if you don't have a 9mm with matching serial numbers to the one that you signed out, then you must stay until it is found. I wonder how long they would actually keep you. I didn't want to find out, so that was one of the first things I got checked back in.

For personal reasons, I kept the uniforms they issued me and paid for their replacements. The Army was issuing a new type of uniform, but I wanted to keep those as mementos. I kept one for me, and one for each of my girls. They still hang in my closet, but maybe someday the girls will like to have them to show to their children. I would love to have my dad's WWII uniform, or a flight uniform from my father-in-law. I guess it's the history buff in me.

As I was out-processing I visited with the commander of CRC and as he was looking over my orders he noticed a slight error. I was supposed to be deployed three hundred and sixty-five days in Afghanistan. My orders read five hundred and forty-five days. When he informed me of that error, I just sat there in disbelief. Not that it would have shortened my stay, because I was there for just under 365 days, but for the military to make such a mistake is unthinkable. It happened though, and we got through it.

ANTICIPATION

On May 12, I received my orders and flight information to return to Tahlequah for reuniting with my family. While waiting for my ride, I heard this voice shout, "Hey, Wilhite, you're home!" I turned and it was Colonel Chris King from West Point. He had redeployed earlier and was returning to Benning to turn in his equipment. A lot of back slapping and joking transpired as we caught up on the current situations, both in Afghanistan and the United States.

The flight home to Tulsa was the third happiest day of my life; marriage and birth of my two girls were bigger days. I arrived home to a great reunion, and after a round of Mexican food, we headed to Tahlequah to begin our adjustment of being a family again.

Almost immediately, Emily and I were summoned to West Point for a presentation that was also going to include a reunion and briefing of those who had been deployed to Afghanistan and to those who were going. It was going to be an exciting time to see my old friends as well as make new ones.

As we arrived on the West Point Campus, I noticed they had a private VIP parking space for me. It read "Colonel James Wilhite, 'Git R Done!'" As mentioned earlier, as I talked about what was needed, I always finished with the comment, "Okay, let's Git R Done!" The Blue Collar Comedy Tour was still alive and well in West Point.

Yes, I am country; yes, I am a redneck; and yes, I like to laugh, mostly at my own expense. It is because of the Blue Comedy Tour that I used the "Git R Done" statement and the reason I called Colonel Tekbas "Scooter."

Many pictures, briefings, dinners, etc. were held while Emily and I were in attendance, but two items I received were very special. One was a certificate appointing me as an Adjunct Faculty Member of West Point, and the other was a beautiful Saber that had the inscription:

"Presented to Colonel James Wilhite,
American Father of the National Military
Academy of Afghanistan from your USMA Colleagues.
Got R Done!"

Mission Complete!

THE SNOWBALL CONTINUES DOWN THE HILL

FOUR YEARS LATER

As I worked around putting something together for this book, I remained in contact with my replacements, Lieutenant Colonel Dean Stroder and Lieutenant Colonel Scott Hamilton. They kept me apprised of what was transpiring throughout their tenure regarding the progress of the academy. Each individual could probably write a book of great interest from their own judgment and perceptions. It has been said there is probably no more documented paperwork relating to any mission that has come from Afghanistan than the vision, design, and implementation of the National Military Academy of Afghanistan.

As the baby was learning to crawl and walk, I was receiving emails from my successors. I had the opportunity to read about their successes as well as their concerns. Both left Afghanistan with similar feelings to what I had. We were proud of what had been accomplished, but were concerned about the continuation of the academy. It was still a fragile baby and the mortality rate in that country is not good.

However, I recently received one of the most detailed summaries about what has happened at the academy since my departure from Colonel Ed Naessens. As you might remember, Colonel Naessens was the first person I worked with after Colonel Shoop and Lieutenant Colonel Wallace redeployed back to the United States. He was there when we were beginning the struggle to build the academy.

Three and one half years later, he returned as the Senior Academic Mentor to the NMAA Academic Support Team, and as he prepared to finish his tour, he sent an excellent documentation of what has happened in the past four years. It is with his permission I submit to you his summary of the National Military Academy of Afghanistan:

FAMILY, FRIENDS, AND COLLEAGUES,

My daughter, Ali, recently asked me about what goes on here at NMAA. I realized that I probably do not send enough information out about what is happening here. I sent her the following, which is probably more than she wanted. I am sending it to you for your information as well; it may be more than you want!

GENERAL OVERVIEW.

I was in Afghanistan four years ago before the first cadets entered the NMAA; now, that I am here four years later, and observed the first cadets graduating, I can tell you, unequivocally, that it is the most profound and satisfying professional experience of my life to see the development of this Academy and what it has accomplished in four short years. We went from a mine-ridden property consisting of an old Soviet Air Academy with no windows and bombed-out infrastructure to the Jewel of Afghanistan in facilities, education, and leader development. The new gymnasium that will be completed in February is the largest gymnasium in Afghanistan. These profound changes have occurred due to the hard work of the Afghan leadership with the mentorship and support of US and coalition forces.

I am the Senior Academic Mentor of the NMAA support team. The team consists of ten base members from multiple services that are assigned to the team anywhere between six months (Air Force) to a year (Army and Navy). The team is augmented in spring, summer and fall sessions with six to twelve faculty members in each session that come from West Point and the United States Air Force Academy (USAFA). These faculty members mentor the Afghans for three to four months before they return to West Point and USAFA.

They mentor and support the Afghan faculty and department heads, the registrar, the brigade tactical department, the physical education program, and the moral/ethical character development program. The team is also augmented with ten Afghan interpreters that have excellent oral and written English language skills. The team also works with ten Turkish officers that provide mentorship to the Afghans in selected areas.

The mission of the NMAA is to educate, train, and inspire the Cadet Brigade so that each graduate is a competent, courageous, and honorable officer in the Afghan National Army, committed to continuous professional development and a lifetime of military and civilian service to the nation.

The NMAA is a true success story in Afghanistan. All instruction, leadership, staff, security, etc. are conducted by Afghans. You will not find a single class taught by anyone other than an Afghan instructor.

The leadership of NMAA consists of an Afghan Superintendent Major General Mohammad Sharif Yaftali. The Afghan Dean is Professor Colonel Hamdullah Yosoufzai. By the way, the Dean's son is a senior cadet at the United States Military Academy at West Point.

He is a civil engineering major. His name is Cadet Shoiab Yosoufzai. He will graduate this May. We are trying to find funding to send him to graduate school in the United States; however, we have not had any luck at this point.* The Commandant of the brigade of cadets is BG Hasamuddin.

The following is a general chronological history (and one future item) of the NMAA:

Aug 03 - Aug 04	MG Eikenberry & USMA Team established foundation for NMAA. BG (Ret) Barney Forsythe instituted the West Point model for the NMAA.
Sep 04 - Feb 05	Accessed first year staff, faculty, and cadets
5 Feb - 20 Mar 05	First Cadet Basic Training conducted
22 Mar 05 year	NMAA Opening Day Ceremony and 1st of academics begins
Jan 06 - Mar 06	First Cadet Advanced Training conducted
25 Mar 06	2nd year of academics began
24 Mar 07	3rd year of academics began
22 Mar 08	4th year of academics began
22 January 09	Class of 2009 NMAA Affirmation Ceremony (celebration of the transition from cadet to officer)
25 January 09	Inaugural graduation of NMAA. Class of 2009 consisting of 84 graduates.
24 March 09	5th year of academics begin, and the first medical students enter (first females cadets-10)
March 2011	NMAA moves to the Afghan Defense University (ADU). Construction is currently planned and on-going for the new Academy.

I like to say just as West Point cadets in 1802 went forth and built a new nation, so too will the graduates of NMAA for the country of

Afghanistan. The NMAA develops officers through a four-year experience integrating four pillars of development: academic, military, physical, and character. NMAA is modeled after West Point. Cadets will leave NMAA with the skill set to be higher-level thinkers prepared to lead the Afghan National Army (and Afghanistan) as leaders of character and competence. Upon graduation, cadets must serve ten years in the Afghan National Army (ANA).

ACADEMIC PROGRAM

The NMAA is the crown jewel of college-level education and leader development in Afghanistan. It is a bachelor degree-producing program that will commission approximately 300 new lieutenants annually that are trained, educated, and inspired in the four pillars of development: academic, military, physical, and character. Graduates will set the highest standards of professionalism throughout a lifetime of service to Afghanistan in military and civilian leadership positions.

My top concern is the credentialing of the faculty. Most of the faculty (over 90%) only have a BS degree from a college/university in Afghanistan. The few MS degrees come from US-contracted faculty (all Afghan) for some of the courses in the majors; however, we will stop providing US-contracted faculty soon. One of my major projects is to get the Ministry of Defense (MOD) and possibly the Ministry of Higher Education (MoHE) to pay for graduate degrees of the faculty in regional colleges/universities. Afghanistan does not have a single college/university that produces MS or higher degrees. Consequently, regional MS degrees can be obtained from India, Pakistan, Turkey, Iran, etc. I do not believe many faculty would be successful attending a Western or European graduate program; they simply do not have the background. Early January we were able to complete the first hurdle to have faculty sent to regional graduate schools! A few more hurdles, and I believe we will begin sending faculty to graduate schools next March!

Although the faculty may not have the credentials, they are very good at what they teach. This is primarily due to the faculty development efforts provided by rotating West Point and USAFA mentors and the hard work by the Afghans to be the best they can in teaching their discipline. Additionally, the NMAA leads the way in Afghanistan in assessing and improving the curriculum.

The Academic program provides the cadets 44 core courses in a broad liberal education. Additionally, cadets get to specialize in an area of interest with twelve (fourteen for civil engineering) courses that constitutes a study in depth (academic major). The broad liberal education provides much more than just learning math, science, engineering, languages, and humanities; rather, it develops critical, creative, and logical thinking skills in every cadet. Additionally, cadets become well grounded in understanding (and not fearing) technology, differences in cultures, academic integrity and moral/ethical behavior, and how to communicate (orally and in writing). Cadets attend classes from 0800 to 1250 every day except Friday. In Afghanistan the weekend starts Thursday afternoon and goes through Friday (or Juma in Afghan) evening.

Consequently, the cadets have class six days a week. The academic year consists of two semesters that last sixteen weeks each. The spring semester begins in March and ends in July. The fall semester begins in September and ends in January.

There are twelve academic departments headed by a Colonel:

- Religion & Culture
- Basic Science consisting of physics, chemistry, biology (new starting in March 2009), and military geography
- Social Science
- Mathematics
- History
- Civil Engineering
- Foreign Language consisting of English, Turkish, French, and German
- Computer Science
- Physical Education
- Law
- Leadership and Management
- Military Science

The cadet daily schedule is as follows:

0630 to 0730	Breakfast & Prayer
0730 to 0745	Morning Parade
0745 to 0800	Move to Class
0800 to 0850	Class (Classes are 50 minutes)
0850 to 0900	Move to Class
0900 to 0950	Class
0950 to 1000	Move to Class
1000 to 1050	Class
1050 to 1100	Move to Class
1100 to 1150	Class
1150 to 1200	Move to Class
1200 to 1250	Class
1250 to 1300	Lunch Information
1300 to 1400	Lunch and Prayer
1400 to 1530	Dean and Commandant Time
1530 to 1800	Intramurals/Drill/Training
1800 to 1810	Dinner Formation
1810 to 1910	Dinner and Prayer
1910 to 2010	Prayer/Personal Time
2010 to 2300	Study
2300	Lights Out

Currently there are four academic majors offered to the cadets. Cadets can choose a civil engineering, computer science, legal studies, or a general engineering and science major. Cadets are capped at seventy-four for the civil engineering and computer science majors due to limited equipment and funding issues. Over the next two years, West Point and the United States Air Force Academy will be working with NMAA to develop two more majors: a leadership and management major, and a language and culture major (English).

Starting this fall, we hope to include an introduction to aeronautical engineering class for those cadets selecting aviation as their branch. Cadets select their branch after their third year.

For the NMAA, every instructor is Afghan. The US (and Turks) mentor the faculty in course development, best practices in how to teach, and how to access accomplishment of objectives in the academic program. Additionally, we mentor the tactical department on military training, leader development, and moral/ethical character development of the cadets. We also mentor the physical education department in physical training, health fitness, and sports.

The NMAA leadership has a keen desire to develop into a Western and European style education. They are always looking to modernize and improve and we are always ready to assist them. We have a true partnership with NMAA. We constantly strive to have the Afghans learn from doing it rather than us doing it for them. They enjoy our partnership and always seek our opinion and recommendation. This same philosophy is the philosophy of US and coalition mentorship throughout all levels of command in the ANA and the Ministry of Defense (MOD).

Starting March 2009, NMAA is going to begin a medical program and provide the MPCB (math, physics, chemistry, and biology) year for medical students. These medical students will spend one year at NMAA to get their foundation in two semesters of calculus, physics, chemistry, and one semester of biology, as well as military science and exposure to the military. These cadets will leave NMAA after their first year and spend the next seven years in medical schools to eventually become doctors in the Afghan National Army. The class of cadets entering this March will have 300 NMAA cadets, plus thirty male medical students, and ten female medical students. This is the first year that NMAA will accept female cadets. Starting in 2011 when NMAA moves to the Afghanistan Defense University in Qargha, the NMAA classes will be increased from 300 cadets to 400 cadets and 10% of the cadet population will be female (other than medical). This is a major accomplishment for the Afghans and their culture. (West Point did not enter its first female cadets until 1980, 178 years after West Point was established.) In Afghanistan, all females must cover their head (scarves); however, less and less are wearing the traditional burkhas. Female instructors and interpreters at NMAA still sit at their own table in the dining facility and they are required to wear head cover (scarves); however, what is interesting is the females soldiers in the ANA are not required to be covered. They are uniformed just like the male soldiers. The ANA and NMAA are very progressive compared to the rest of the Afghan culture. The female cadets at NMAA will undergo the same training, education, and inspirational development that the male cadets will receive; however, the females will be housed in separate barracks and they will not be combined with males in sporting and physical events. The NMAA leadership is genuinely excited at having female cadets at NMAA. A couple weeks ago I attended the opening ceremony of a woman soldier education center for the ANA. The ANA is increasing the size of its Army with a corresponding increase in the female soldier population.

MILITARY PROGRAM

The brigade of cadets consists of four battalions of three companies each. Each company consists of three platoons and each platoon consists of three squads. The total cadet population starting in March 2009 will be approximately 1150 cadets. In addition to four years of military science in the academic program, the military program progressively develops cadets over four years from followers to leaders. During the academic year military training also focuses on:

- Ethics, values, honor training
- Leadership development seminars
- Motivational guest speakers
- Counseling

Daily unit training time, after academics, is used for drill and ceremony, company athletics, and/or company-level training. The four year summer training program (July through October each year) focuses on developing military skills as well as leadership skills and decision-making.

1) Cadet Basic Training (CBT) is the first year: (There are two CBT periods)

Cadet Basic Training I (CBT I) at NMAA

- Fifteen days prior to the beginning of the academic year in March.
- Training includes values, ethics, and honor, introduction to the
- Afghan National Army, map reading, first aid, drill and ceremonies

223

- Cadet Basic Training II (CBT II) at Kabul Military Training Center (KMTC)

- Training focuses on individual and collective common task training

- The leader development focus is to learn how to be a follower.

2) Cadet Advanced Training (CAT) is the second year:

- Training includes advanced first aid, land navigation, weapons qualification

- The focus is at squad battle drills

- The leader development focus is to learn how to be a member of a team and to be a Team Leader.

3) Cadet Orientation Training is the third year: (Learn the value of a noncommissioned officer, NCO)

- *Training includes heavy weapons training, field artillery, combat engineering, logistics, and signal training

- The focus is at platoon level operations

- The leader development focus is to learn the value of the NCO.

4) Cadet Troop Leader Training is the Fourth year:

- Training is focused on cadets being officers as they serve as platoon leaders and company commanders.

CBT II and CAT chain of command.

The leader development focus is to learn how officers lead.

PHYSICAL PROGRAM

The physical program does much more than develop cadets to be physically fit and healthy. The program is focused on developing a warrior spirit through sports. Cadets take two years of physical education in the academic program and participate in intramural sports all four years.

During time off you will see many cadets working out in the gymnasium, the pull up bars, jogging or playing soccer.

I am trying to get lacrosse equipment to teach them how to play lacrosse. It is quite cold in Afghanistan in the winter months; however, it is not cold enough to sustain an ice rink so that I can teach them ice hockey!**

CHARACTER DEVELOPMENT PROGRAM

The character development program focuses on the developing cadets sense of duty, honor, commitment to country in which the moral/ethical development is grounded in their Islamic faith. The cadet's live by the motto: God, Duty, Country.

Some aspects of the program:

- Cadet Honor System was planned and approved Dec 2008; full cadet program will be implemented for the new academic year beginning March 2009.

- Brigade Tactical Officers and staff members have received intense honor code and honor system training; seminars will continue for all faculty and cadets so that they can develop, inspire, and train other cadets.

- The Brigade of Cadets will have company, battalion, and brigade honor representatives (3rd and 4th year cadets) effective March 2009

- Cadets receive professional military ethics training at the company level and during their military studies curriculum

- Faculty and staff receive professional military ethics training during Dean and

- Commandant's hours in the afternoons between 2:00 PM and 3:30 PM.

- Motivational and Inspirational speaker speak to the cadets, staff, and faculty throughout the academic year

The programs described above are getting better and so are the cadets. Future graduating classes will demonstrate the true value of NMAA as an institution skilled at developing cadets as leaders of character and competence.

THE CADETS

The following outlines how many cadets were considered at admission, of those how many were accepted, and how many are in the current class. As you can see the interest is increasing for attendance at NMAA. As the word spread in Afghanistan, it will continue to increase. One problem in Afghanistan is the lack of internet, land line telephones, and road/ rail networks. Communication across Afghanistan is very difficult. We use ANA recruiting stations throughout all the provinces as the source to spread the word and seek candidates for admission to NMAA. Additionally, the support we received from the President of Afghanistan at the graduation will go a long way in providing a great future for the Academy.

Number of Admissions

Year	Applicants	(Accepted/Current)
Class of 2009	360	120/84
Class of 2010	1007	270/215
Class of 2011	1195	386/312
Class of 2012	1789	310/289
Class of 2013	2200+	330 +/ 40
Medical	(30 male/10 female)	

There are thirty-four provinces and five ethnic distributions in Afghanistan. Great care is taken to ensure the NMAA is comprised of cadets from all of Afghanistan's major ethnic groups: Pashtu, Tajik, Uzbek, Hazara, Turkmen, etc., and balanced according to the country's national averages. They also try to ensure cadets are represented from all thirty-four provinces in Afghanistan. Currently, there are cadets from every province in Afghanistan.

The ethnic distribution for the cadets is

- Pashtu 37%
- Tajik 35%
- Hazara 12%
- Uzbek 8%
- Other 8%

These percentages roughly match the country of Afghanistan. The faculty and staff are required to be within the windows of the ethnic distribution as well. The Faculty and staff distribution is:

- Pashtu 41%
- Tajik 40%
- Hazara 6%
- Uzbek 5%
- Other 8%

It is very competitive to become a cadet. NMAA conducts a three-day admissions event at NMAA where cadet candidates from all provinces and ethnicities are selected based on the results of a Concord Exam (like our SAT or ACT exam in the US) and a Physical Fitness Test.

Cadets selected to attend NMAA must then pass a medical fitness examination. Cadets cannot be older than twenty-three and they cannot be married. In the most recent admissions three-day event there were over 2200 candidates and only 330 were selected to become cadets and forty selected as medical students (thirty male and ten female).

THE AFGHAN NATIONAL ARMY AND AIR CORPS.

The Afghan National Army (ANA) is receiving tremendous mentorship, equipment, and training from US and other coalition forces. The Afghan officers, noncommissioned officers, and soldiers attend basic training and developmental schools that are modeled after US and other coalition schools. In 2002, when I was in Afghanistan with CJTF-Mountain during Operation Anaconda, there was no ANA; however, the Afghan Northern Alliance and tribal militias fought alongside of us. Today, in seven short years, there is a vibrant Afghan National Army that is getting stronger and better equipped every day.

The ANA has gone from old former Soviet Union equipment to using and training on United States and coalition modern weapon systems. Every Afghan recruit receives entry and advance skills training at either the Kabul Military Training Center or the Regional Basic Warrior Training Center. The ANA is comprised of soldiers from all of Afghanistan's major ethnic groups and balanced according to the country's national averages.

The ANA is truly a national army, representing all the people of Afghanistan. The ANA is primarily a light-infantry-based army equipped with towed artillery and mortars. The ANA is trained and mentored by coalition forces to be able to take the lead in securing and defending unilaterally the independence, national sovereignty and territorial integrity against all enemies, foreign and domestic. The Afghan National Air Corps is an important element of the ANA. Equipped with former Soviet Union aircraft, fixed and rotary wing, the Afghan National Air Corp (ANAC) is being trained to perform a wide range of missions that include Presidential airlift, medical and casualty evacuation, battlefield mobility, air lift, reconnaissance and airborne command and control, and light air attack. They are recently building the ANAC with US and coalition air frames to include US UH-1 or Huey helicopters. It is interesting to note that twenty of the NMAA cadets graduating this January along with twenty-eight ANA Soldiers form the ANA were selected for the pilot program. They will undergo intensive English-speaking education before they depart to the US for flight school. Since Afghanistan is a land-locked country there are no naval forces!

The first graduating class provided eighty-four graduates to the ANA. Out of these eighty-four cadets they are branched in the ANA as follows:

- Infantry 24

- Armor 7

- Artillery 13

- Aviation 20 (will attend US Army aviation school)

- Logistics 13
- Signal 7

There is no branch of engineers; however, they are currently developing this branch and we expect to commission cadets in the engineers next year. For the eighteen civil engineer cadets that are graduating this January, many of them will gain practical engineering experience working with the Afghanistan Engineering District (US Army Engineer organization) to build facilities for Afghanistan. Additionally, some of the engineers will go to ANA Corps level installations to do engineer facilities work.

I hope this will give you a better picture of the great strides that have been accomplished in this country.

—Ed

*Note: Funding was received and Shoiab will be going to Graduate School at the University of Nebraska, Omaha.

**Note: Colonel Naessens is the faculty representative for West Point Hockey. He also coaches the Mighty Mites age five and under hockey team. It is worth a trip to visit West Point just to watch him interact with the children in their hockey gear.

CONCLUSION

A s you can see from the final chapter, a lot has happened to the National Military Academy of Afghanistan since its birth on February 5, 2005. It is probably one of the most documented events that has transpired in that country, yet very little is known about it. Please read and spread the word about the good news that can come from a war-torn country.

This is only one of many acts of the United States and coalition forces that have made impacts in education, medicine, roads, and equally important attitudes in the Afghan people.

This is not about the guns and gore of war in a country that has experienced such issues over the past twenty-five to thirty years. It is a feel-good story that brought active, reserve, and IRR soldiers together for a common cause, to assist in the development of a safe and productive country in Afghanistan.

Yes, we had rocket attacks, yes we had IEDs, yes, we had soldiers killed and you probably read about each event as it happened.

What you didn't hear about was the great accomplishments that were conducted by the United States Military and the NATO Forces. Their ability to work together was remarkable and should be recognized.

This specific mission of building the National Military Academy was supported not only by the coalition forces, but also by citizens of the United States. They sent many boxes of supplies for the troops and the school. It was truly a total combined effort.

As I developed this book I realized that I was just a small part of the puzzle. I was called the glue that kept it together and didn't allow the mission to fall apart. I guess a puzzle is no good without the glue, especially if you want to keep it together for a long time.

I have always believed that God put us on this earth for a reason. It took many years for me to figure that out, but when I did it made my life much more meaningful. I have told my students that I felt I was placed on this earth to teach, to make a difference in someone's life regardless of their age. I have always loved teaching, and that is what I believe my calling is.

We are tested throughout our lifetime for our commitment to be here. I thought I was tested with the deployment into a war zone. However, as you read throughout the book, you will notice that opportunities were presented to me that I can say were no less than divine intervention. Someone had a hand in it, and I grew to believe that hand was the hand of God.

I remember stepping out one winter morning from breakfast and stopping for a minute to look around and do some reflecting. I was by myself and had a few minutes to meditate as to my being there. All of a sudden I got this cold chill and a slight rigor throughout my body. I was not cold when this happened either.

The NMAA was a given and was going to be a reality. I could see the light at the end of the tunnel, and it was not another train. I started to smile a goofy smile, and about that time, a young soldier came up to me and asked if I was okay. I nodded calmly and said, "Yes, I am fine because I finally know why I am here." I walked off to the bewilderment of the young soldier and a feeling of accomplishment as to my service while in Afghanistan.

That was it. I was there for my service. My service to teach, my service to build, my service to make a difference, my opportunity to put everything I had worked toward in education and military training to one mission that would benefit others.

Many people in the United States take for granted the freedoms and material things they have. I returned home with a significantly better appreciation for everything I have been blessed to receive. The Afghan faculty did not have the best of equipment, facilities, or funding, but they did possess something that we seem to miss when we are in similar situations: a positive attitude! They took what they had and learned how to better it. It is said, "We did so much with so little, we now feel that we can do almost anything with nothing." I witnessed that firsthand, and as mentioned already, it all seemed to evolve around "attitude." Their attitudes were contagious and were definitely worth catching. An opportunity was presented to them and their students for a great education and possible better life, and they were not going to let that opportunity get past them.

Yes, we answered the call to build the Crown Jewel of Afghanistan. It was not one person; it was a collective effort by many people and many nations, but most importantly by the Afghans themselves. Now it will be the graduates of the NMAA who will answer the call to serve their country and be the future soldiers, leaders, and scholars of their people now and for future generations.

Inshala!

I n October 2009, the Minister of Defense (MoD), GEN Wardak, and the Minister of Higher Education (MoHE), Deputy Mohammad Azam Dadfar, met to sign a protocol between MoHE and MoD acknowledging NMAA as an institute of higher education. During the ceremony Deputy Dadfar officially acknowledged NMAA as the 22nd college or university in Afghanistan. In addition to being acknowledged by MoHE, NMAA can now begin to seek accreditation of majors and agrees to work closely with MoHE to advance the academic programs. The protocol certainly advances the status of NMAA throughout Afghanistan. MG Sharif was on center stage during the ceremony and the event was attended by the National media and most to the principals from the General Staff. The news of the protocol spread quickly in the cadet brigade. The NMAA is no longer considered just a military school but also an academic institution.

FINAL NOTE:

Since returning home I have attended many programs where shows end in some sort of patriotic song. As they sing they ask all veterans to stand and be recognized for their service and there is generally a thunderous applause. While that is most appreciated, I ask that organizations like that also have the spouses and children stand for recognition. They are the heroes of the home front and I am forever grateful for what my wife and children, along with what other families had to endure while their spouses have been deployed. It doesn't make any difference if it is Operation Enduring Freedom, Operation Iraqi Freedom, Viet Nam, Korea, World War II or anything in between. We should always recognize our family support just as much as we are recognized. God Bless our families and God Bless America!